W9-DJP-793

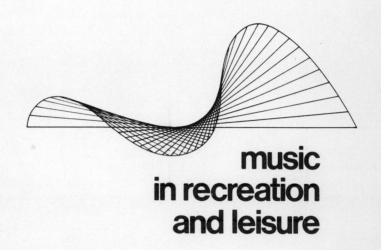

music
in recreation
and leisure

MT
87
B4

119815

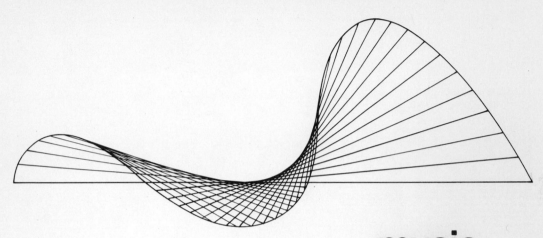

music
in recreation
and leisure

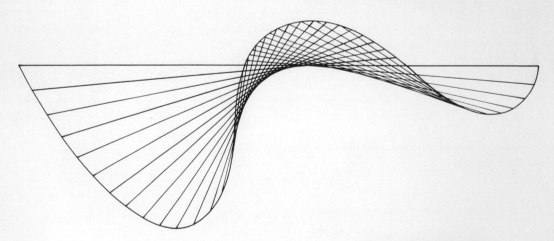

JOHN BATCHELLER
University of New Mexico, Albuquerque

SALLY MONSOUR
Georgia State University, Atlanta

WM. C. BROWN COMPANY PUBLISHERS, DUBUQUE, IOWA **wcb**

GOSHEN COLLEGE LIBRARY
GOSHEN, INDIANA 46526

Consulting Editor
Frederick W. Westphal
Sacramento State College

Copyright © 1972 by Wm. C. Brown Company Publishers

Library of Congress Catalog Card Number: 71—190195

ISBN 0—697—03486—0

All rights reserved. No part of this publication may be reproduced, stored in a retrieval system, or transmitted, in any form or by any means, electronic, mechanical, photocopying, recording, or otherwise, without the prior written permission of the copyright owner.

Printed in the United States of America

We call you to join man's race to maturity, to work with us in inventing the future. We believe that a human adventure is just beginning: that mankind has so far been restricted in developing its innovative and creative powers because it was overwhelmed by toil. Now we are free to be as human as we will.

— Ivan D. Illich

contents

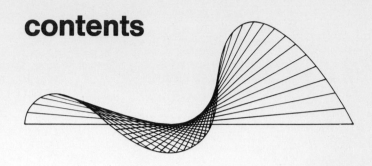

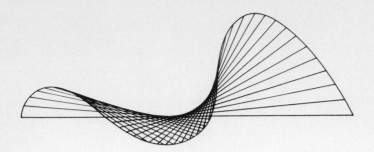

preface

This book is a practical guide to the ways and means of planning music programs for both leisure and recreation. It is intended for program directors in the several areas of music in community recreation, camping, industry, senior citizens, correctional institutions, armed services, pleasure cruisers, and clinical institutions. In all of these areas, music should have an important place.

The authors believe that all persons connected with recreation or leisure programs should know something about music. This is true of administrators as well as persons actually conducting musical activities. In this regard, it is important to know the bases upon which music assumes importance in the lives of persons from both a social and a psychological point of view. It is also valuable to have descriptions of programs which are in operation and ideas about how such programs were initiated. Finally, it is necessary to know instructional techniques and resources for implementing programs. Helpful hints and practical procedures can often make the difference between a program that functions successfully and one that does not.

This book is organized into an introduction followed by three main parts. The introduction is generally devoted to the need for music in a projected life style. Included in this are the ingredients of a good program. Following the introduction are suggestions for musical activities in various recreational settings. Incorporated into each part is a discussion of the place of music and a general description of program content. Materials are sometimes suggested and model programs reviewed. Finally, the book contains instructional ideas and teaching resources. Here, the authors chose to include such related experiences as group singing and song leadership, instrumental accompaniment, sound exploration, choral speaking, and dramatic movement and traditional dancing. There are, of course, many other instructional activities—limited only by the recreation leader's resourcefulness and imagination.

The authors wholeheartedly support the view that music is a source of inspiration through which one can be happily occupied. In other words, music can help to create a positive environment directly related to our well-being. It is with a dedicated awareness of the particular need for music in mankind's continuing and dynamic societal evolution that this book is presented.

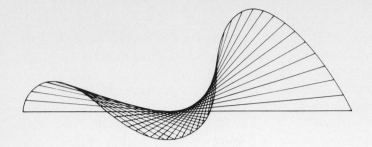

introduction

PRELIMINARY IDEAS

The recurrent theme of social change within a "post-industrial" society seems to be the need for using our creative energies. From a historical point of view, this need is both crucial and immediate. The change explosion is rapid and only partially predictable. The communication explosion alone is an illustration.

> Imagine a clock face with sixty minutes on it. Let the clock stand for the time men have had access to writing systems. Our clock would thus represent something like 3,000 years, and each minute on our clock fifty years. On this scale, there were no significant media changes until about nine minutes ago. At that time, the printing press came into use in Western culture. About three minutes ago: the telegraph, photograph, and locomotive arrived. Two minutes ago: the telephone, rotary press, motion pictures, automobile, airplane and radio. One minute ago, the talking picture. Television has appeared in the last ten seconds, the computer in the last five, and communications satellites in the last second. The laser beam—perhaps the most potent medium of communication of all—appeared only a fraction of a second ago.[1]

Rapid changes are also reflected in the amount of leisure time we now enjoy. The average wage earner already has 4,000 free hours a year. According to the American Association of Health, Physical Education and Recreation,

> Well over 3,000 communities in the United States spend a total of a billion dollars a year on public recreation to help him fill those hours usefully and enjoyably. As much as 40 billion dollars is spent annually for all types of recreation. Prospects for the future clearly point toward even more leisure and even more income—both public and private—for recreation purposes.[2]

Man's problems relative to the quality of his life style will certainly reflect these rapid alterations in job patterns, work schedules, and income. It was with this in mind that the newly established Institute for Studies of Leisure made its first public statement in 1968 by listing such issues as:

> The human impacts of cybernation, economic and political transformations (such as the guaranteed annual income), a philosophy for abundant time and increasing affluence,

---

1. Neil Postman and Charles Weingartner, *Teaching as a Subversive Activity* (New York: Delacorte Press, 1969), p. 10.
2. *Recreation as Your Career*, AAHPER (Washington, D.C.: National Education Association).

classlessness in consuming patterns, extension of significant nonwork commitments, more thrusts of adult education, principles for counseling in the use of new time-bulks, preparation for retirement, and so on.

The Institute went on to question the nature of new leisure for the middle classes; how leisure is related to the questions of young people; where new values are coming from to meet new conditions of affluence, time, mobility, and mass media.[3]

Such emerging issues will require our best efforts at solving the problems of leisure and recreation. Music and the other arts will, by their nature, supply us with avenues through which these problems may be solved.

Music can be woven into practically every phase of leisure and the quality of life. It is expressive as well as creative. Music affords performing outlets on practically every level and for every occasion. The re-creative benefits of music are numerous. One has only to review the place music could have in the following ranked listing of elements making up the quality of living. These elements and their ranking resulted from a National Conference on the Quality of Life in a Leisure-Centered Society held at La Costa, California in March, 1970.[4] Note that a major portion of the experiences that really count in life are contributed by leisure.

Musical activities can serve as fulfilling agents for each of these qualities. For this reason, the authors have inserted an additional column relating each quality to a musical activity.

LEISURE AND THE QUALITY OF LIFE

QUALITY	MUSICAL ACTIVITY	PRIORITY RANK ORDER	IMPORTANCE (0-100)	CONTRIBUTION BY LEISURE (0-100)
Self-respect (Self-confidence, self-understanding)	Solo performance, contribution within a group, ethnic programs	1	100	54
Achievement (Sense of accomplishment, meaningful activity)	Harmonizing by ear, learning to read music, selected for talent shows	2	98	59
Health (Physical well-being, feeling good)	Posture, coordination through movement and dance	3	96	68
Affection (Love, caring, relating, understanding)	Campfire sings, all forms of *group* music making	4	93	61

3. Newsletter of the Institute for Studies of Leisure, Vol. I, No. 1, May, 1969. Inquiries about the work of the Institute may be addressed to Prof. Max Kaplan, Director, Institute for Studies of Leisure, University of South Florida, Tampa, Florida 33620.

4. Report issued from the Conference on Leisure and the Quality of Life, co-sponsored by the American Association for Health, Physical Education and Recreation (AAHPER) and the American Institute of Planners (AIP). Further information may be obtained from Dr. Donald Hawkins, Consultant in Recreation, AAHPER (1201 16th Street, N.W., Washington, D. C. 20036).

LEISURE AND THE QUALITY OF LIFE

QUALITY	MUSICAL ACTIVITY	PRIORITY RANK ORDER	IMPORTANCE (0-100)	CONTRIBUTION BY LEISURE (0-100)
Freedom (Individuality, spontaneity, unconstrained)	Exploring rhythms and movements, sound exploration and composition	5	91	71
Involvement (Participation, concern)	Group music-making	6	89	63
Challenge (Stimulation, competition, ambition)	Musical shows, competitions, festivals	7	84	56
Security (Peace of mind, stability, lack of conflict)	Group music-making	8	82	51
Comfort (Economic well-being, good things, relaxation)	Listening to music	9	61	50
Status (Prestige, social recognition, positive feedback)	Song leading, harmonizing by ear, talent awards	10	52	37
Novelty (Newness, surprise variety)	Sound exploration, composition	11	49	50
Dominance (Superiority, power, control, aggression)	Song leadership, musical director, solo performance	12	26	26

ELEMENTS OF A GOOD PROGRAM OF MUSIC IN RECREATION

Elements for a good program reflect the need for enjoyment, self-fulfillment, understanding, and sympathetic leadership. Also needed are informed directors who are aware of the cultural and artistic aspects of living. While pleasure and enjoyment are heavily stressed, this point must not be interpreted as ignoring the acknowledged benefits of quality and depth. A single musical experience is capable of affording great pleasure and enjoyment to those involved. It can, at the same time, be an experience of modest musical proportions. By the same token, persons involved in a profound or complex musical experience may also receive a like portion of enjoyment. The intention is to place the stress of recreational music on pleasure and enjoyment first, rather than on an overserious effort to create a perfect production. With these points in mind, selected elements to a good program, equally important might be:

1. All activities offered to any group should produce pleasure.
2. Participants should experience enjoyment and a certain fulfillment of their aesthetic and creative natures.
3. Experiences should be emphasized which are not generally a part of everyday routine.
4. Time should be available in which a person could develop a newly discovered musical outlet.

5. Experiences should be offered which will enable a person to nurture his own aptitudes in various musical ways.
6. Adequate equipment should be available which affords more than make-shift approaches to the creation of an authentic musical climate.
7. Directors, supervisors, and leaders should be aware of the importance of music as an integral part of mankind's need for self-discovery, self-expression, and self-enhancement.
8. Musical experiences should have a direct and positive influence on the immediate environment in which they take place.
9. Excess time and undue pressures should be eliminated so that maximum enjoyment can be maintained.
10. Undesirable and destructive practices designed for technical perfection and performing exploitation must be avoided.

QUALITIES FOR MUSIC LEADERSHIP IN RECREATION PROGRAMS

One imperative for an effective and functioning music recreation program is the music leader who is given the responsibility for its development and implementation. The recreation leader must have the personal qualities and training which are important for all music teachers. In addition he should have special competencies which will be valuable in recreational or leisure-time situations. The combination of these expectant competencies are listed in Table 1.

DEVELOPMENT OF MUSICAL FEELING AND SENSITIVITY

In essence, music contains many unique characteristics which are often listed as elements, i.e., pitch, duration, texture, color, and form. While not all recreation programs are concerned with developing a high degree of knowledge of these elements, there should always be an attempt to create a sensitive musical environment in which a feeling for these elements may be experienced. For purposes of clarity and usefulness in the context of this book, the following outline includes an intellectual breakdown of musical elements in descriptive terms.

FEELING FOR. . .	THROUGH	SENSITIVITY TO. . .
1. Rhythm		Beat, accent, tempo, phrase, pattern, silent motion.
2. Linear Movement and Horizontal Line		General shape, direction, phrase, interval, register, rhythm pattern.
3. Quality of Sound		Sound variance, grouping, texture, source.
4. Vertical Textures		Two or more simultaneous rhythmic or melodic lines, relation of harmony to melody, combinations of tonal qualities.
5. Tension and Release		Phrase, climax, dynamics, rubato, texture.
6. Beginning and Ending		Repetition, alteration, change, contrast, pattern, part vs. whole.

TABLE 1

EXPECTED COMPETENCIES FOR MUSIC TEACHERS AND LEADERS IN RECREATION

ALL TEACHERS SHOULD BE ABLE TO	IN ADDITION. . . . MUSIC TEACHERS SHOULD BE ABLE TO	IN ADDITION. . . . MUSIC LEADERS IN RECREATION SHOULD BE ABLE TO
demonstrate a knowledge of physical, emotional, and intellectual development	select the most effective methods for helping each student achieve maximum musical awareness and satisfaction	arrange simple music for various musical combinations
integrate the isolated facts of human development into a substantial framework for influencing behavior	evaluate musical backgrounds, interests, attitudes, and abilities of students.	demonstrate the ability to accompany songs and improvise accompaniments on at least one instrument
master the psychological data basic to an understanding of the many facets of human learning	communicate artistic concepts of musical styles and periods	make simple musical instruments
establish an environment which is appropriate to the goals of learners and their needs	demonstrate proficiency regarding the theoretical aspects of a score	create a learning environment which reflects creativity and discovery
radiate a healthy adjustment to the problems of living	perform acceptably on at least one musical instrument	articulate a working knowledge of social elements within a musical group
	conduct clearly and expressively	communicate ideas regarding the role of music in the school and in the culture
	detect and diagnose musical problems in both aural and written form	influence others regarding the unique value of music in human living and inspire them to respond to music in positive ways
		demonstrate flexibility and imagination in meeting new situations

musical examples index

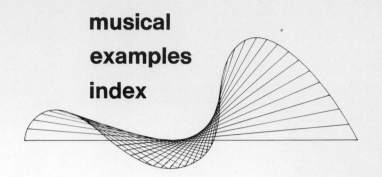

xvii

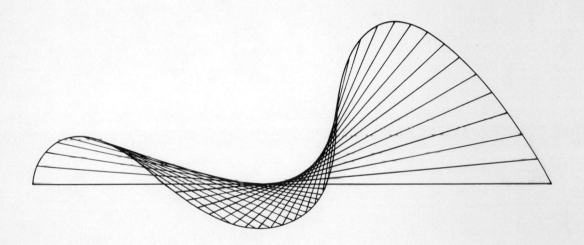

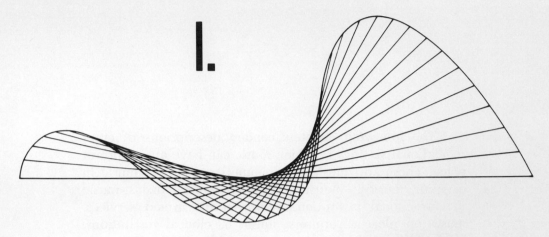

I.

music in
recreation
programs

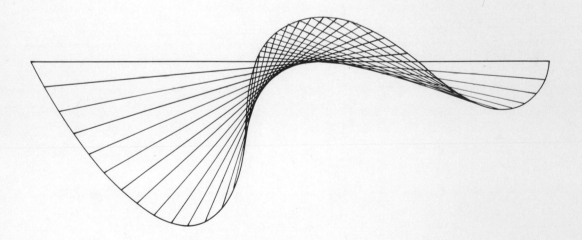

The following chapters contain descriptions of eight recreational settings in which music can have an important place. These are: music in community recreation, music in camping, music in industry, music for senior citizens, music in correctional institutions, music in the armed services, music on pleasure cruisers, music in clinical institutions. Each category of recreation contains a discussion of the role of music and several suggestions for musical activities.

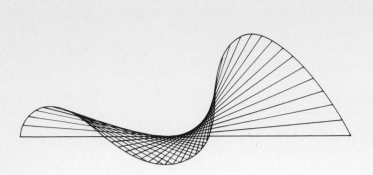

1.

music in community recreation

Music washes away from the soul the dust of everyday life.

Auerbach

Recreation is a vital concern in most communities—both rural and urban. Because of this, municipal governments allot specific funds to support recreation programs. This support ranges from the hiring of trained recreation leaders to the maintenance of community recreation buildings.

Depending upon the size of the community, some type of leadership is definitely required to organize and direct a well-balanced and comprehensive public recreation program. Both the leadership and staff of these programs should be aware of the increasing need for meaningful leisure in society as a whole. They should also know those concepts and ideals relative to the social units they serve. A reciprocal challenge faces the community itself which must lend its firm support to the basic principles of adequate public recreation.

The recreation director will have the ultimate responsibility for initiating ideas relative to the program. He must also see them through in terms of their success. It is hoped that the following guidelines will provide a basis for awareness by those who are directly responsible for planning and maintaining community recreation programs.

1. **An aware director** recognizes that every community has a multitude of cultural resources. One such cultural resource includes persons living in the community who are members of various ethnic groups. These people are invaluable to the music program by sharing their knowledge of and experience with their own folk music. *Recreational music activities need these resources for enrichment and interest.*
2. **An aware director** includes activities based on the needs and abilities of the people in the community. *Music is a need for all and an interest for many.*
3. **An aware director** knows that a good community recreation program is something far beyond a series of specialized events. *A program without some directed emphasis on music would not be sufficiently broad and well-balanced.*
4. **An aware director** has a healthy, realistic understanding of the importance of worthwhile leisure activities. Not everyone is able to participate in sports in his leisure hours, *but everyone can enjoy music on an individual or group basis.*
5. **An aware director** has the ability to utilize the natural beauty of the community in the recreation program. *Many musical functions are enriched by the beauty of the setting in which they take place.*

6. **An aware director** believes in man's unique creative powers and knows that a recreation program should provide opportunities for a variety of creative experiences. *Music offers all levels of creativity from actual composition to creative listening.*

7. **An aware director** is conscious of music's place in the recreational life of people. *Enlisting the talents of local musicians is one way to augment the music activities of a community recreation program.*

8. **An aware director** has the patience and energy to continually evaluate the existing program to be certain it includes activities for all the young, the old, the average, the slow, the gifted, the spectator, and the doer. *The unique qualities of music allow for its universal inclusiveness in community recreation programs.*

9. **An aware director** knows that a worthwhile community recreation program requires equipment and space. Special effort is therefore needed to locate the appropriate resources for musical activities. These include instruments, books, recording and playback equipment, sheet music, tapes, and scores.

MUSICAL ACTIVITIES AND THE RECREATION CENTER

The musical activities included in a program of community recreation will naturally vary with the needs of each situation. Rural and urban centers will reflect differences, as will centers located in the midst of ethnic social units. Variance in staff and financial support will also determine the kind of program that becomes an actuality.

Despite these variances, however, most programs reflect the interests and needs of persons who are seeking recreation and refreshment during their leisure hours. The age groups will represent a cross section of both young and old. Human interests and hobbies will conceivably encompass an unimaginable array of sponsored activities. Some of these will come and go according to local interest. Others will remain as a consistent offering throughout the years. In this regard, music generally finds a place of essential importance.

In order to meet the physical needs of a multi-activity program, most communities set aside public space designated as a recreation center ("rec" center). Enclosed buildings are common, together with the adjunct facilities of out-of-door shelters, playgrounds, and parks. Regardless of the facility, it is the quality of the activities themselves that usually determines the success of the program offered to the people. The social nature of music and the multiple expressions through which it is experienced, both formally and informally, make it a worthwhile activity within a community recreation setting.

The precise nature and structure of a community program can be as extensive as the imaginations of the directing staff will allow. The following list of activities represents the ideas of many successful recreation leaders. These activities may be expanded according to the unique setting of individual situations. Some may not even apply and should, therefore, be discarded or altered.

Guidelines for Musical Activities in Community Recreation Programs

1. Sponsor classes in instrument playing, such as class piano, chord organ, uke-guitar, recorder, etc.
2. Promote community singing programs. These may be in the form of "sing alongs" or community singing ensembles and groups.
3. Institute a "Music Day" as a part of a local fair or festival.
4. Assist in the functions of a community chorus, band, or orchestra.
5. Encourage and sponsor community-wide amateur contests which appeal to all levels of musical talent.

6. Sponsor classes in folk dancing for all age groups.
7. Sponsor out-of-doors park concerts and pageants.
8. Develop a community record loan library.
9. Incorporate music activities and classes into the summer park recreation program.
10. Establish a civic opera which would combine many musical elements.
11. Inaugurate a "Music Week Festival." This could involve all elements of the music program during National Music Week (begins the first Sunday in May).
12. Add "live" music (and musical events) as an adjunct to city skating rink competitions or swimming pool water ballet programs.
13. Plan and present both formal lectures and informal discussion groups dealing with various aspects of music in today's society. Prominent local musicians can be asked to conduct these sessions. This type of musical activity can find a spot on the agenda of the recreation center. People who neither play nor sing are often interested in topics about music.
14. Sponsor teenage dances featuring both local and well-known instrumental groups.
15. Plan activities involving the making of musical instruments. These may be simple in the case of very young children, or elaborate enough to include dulcimers, tub basses, one-stringed fiddles, etc.
16. Sponsor public performances by jug bands, musical saws, etc.
17. Set aside a music room in the center. Included should be music playback equipment for listening (with earphones), and a selection of books and magazines about music for reading purposes.[1] Listening programs may be scheduled and tapes of the center's music programs can be listened to.

ETHNIC FESTIVALS

One of the most popular and meaningful events sponsored by community recreation is an ethnic festival. Exposure to the national character of a group of people often brings with it better knowledge and therefore understanding of our common hopes and aspirations, as well as the distinctive differences among human beings. These festivals have appeal for all age groups. They provide a vehicle for musical folk expression which is always interesting regardless of the level of the talent involved.

Local consulates, residents, and libraries are the primary sources for information relative to an ethnic festival. Newspaper "calls for information" are an excellent way to locate persons who have special talents and information about other cultures and customs. Songs, dances, and recitations usually form the basis for such festivals. Designated dates of significance in the particular culture represented are the most usual times for such festivals to take place. These are most often on the dates of independence.

TEEN CENTERS

A rapidly growing aspect of community recreation, especially in larger cities is the teen center. These are sometimes located in separate facilities or are a part of such programs as boys and girls clubs.

The major emphasis in these centers is personal involvement for social development and aesthetic satisfaction. These goals are achieved with the aid of spirited and enthusiastic leaders who are dedicated to the ideals of current psychological thought.

1. See Appendix C for list of *Books about Music for Libraries,* p. 114.

Programs and activities especially suited to these goals are:

Accordion Lessons
Banjo Lessons
Bell Choirs
Boys' Choruses
Combos for Dancing
Folk and Ethnic Music Festivals
Folk Singing
Guitar Lessons
Harmonica Lessons
Jam Session (Rock and Folk)
Jazz Clubs
Jug, Bottle, and Fife Groups
Kazoo Bands
Kitchen Bands
Musical Programs for Shopping Centers
Piano Lessons
Recorder (Tonette) Lessons
Stunt Shows
Talent Shows
Ukulele Lessons

SELECTED REFERENCES

BENGTSSON, ARVID. *Environmental Planning for Children's Play.* New York: Praeger, 1970.
BUTLER, GEORGE, D. *Playgrounds: Their Administration and Operation.* New York: McGraw-Hill, 1940.
———. *Recreation Areas—Their Design and Equipment.* New York: Ronald Press, 1958.
Community Organization for Recreation. Papers presented at the 9th Annual Institute in Recreation Administration, 1964. Washington, D. C.: National Recreation and Park Association.
DOELL, CHARLES. *Elements of Park and Recreation Administration.* Available from National Recreation and Park Administration, Washington, D. C.
EGBERT, MARION. "Music Is What's Happening." *Parks and Recreation.* (June, 1970):22-24, 57-60.
FRIESWYK, SIEBOLT. *Mobile and Portable Recreation Facilities in Parks and Recreation.* Available from National Recreation and Park Association, Washington, D. C.
GUGGENHEIMER, ELINOR C. *Planning for Parks and Recreation Needs in Urban Areas.* New York: Twayne, 1969.
LEDERMANN, ALFRED, and TRACHSEL, ALFRED. *Creative Playgrounds and Recreation Centers.* Available from National Recreation and Park Association, Washington, D. C.
McCARTY, THEODORE. "Making Music." *Parks and Recreation.* (April, 1971):25-26, 62-63.
RODNEY, LYNNE S. *Administration of Public Recreation.* New York: Ronald Press, 1964.
ROTUNNO, MARTIN. "A Statistical Study to Examine the Amount of Knowledge Effected by Recreation Experiences in Music." Unpublished master's thesis. University of Illinois, 1961.

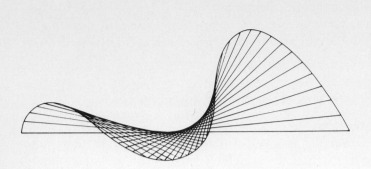

2.

music in camping

Join we now as friends, and celebrate the brotherhood we share. Keep the fires burning and we'll all join in and sing.

Summer camps, both public and private, are a firmly established American tradition, and there are thousands of them now in operation. They are generally sponsored by organizations or by individuals who are committed to the life of the out-of-doors. Some are established for profit-making, while others are organized by service organizations, religious groups, or altruistic individuals.

There are also camps devoted exclusively to the study and performance of music and are naturally patronized by students with musical talent. These resemble a music school or out-of-doors conservatory where music is a serious pursuit and is not considered recreational in the traditional sense. In recreational settings nothing over-planned or tightly scheduled is able to produce the "magic" environment which music is capable of casting over life at camp.

MUSIC LEADERSHIP IN CAMPS

It is generally agreed that it is the campers themselves who should eventually do the music leading. Camp counselors and recreational music leaders should devise programs that will permit this kind of leadership development. The music camp leader's primary duty is to guide and assist. In short, a wise leader "gets out of the picture" as soon as musical events and programs are organized. Here are some characteristics of a good music counselor.

He should:

1. Be a person open to suggestions.
2. Be a person able to follow through on a suggestion so that it becomes a successful experience.
3. Be a person able to recognize a good idea when he hears one.
4. Be a person with an extensive repertoire of songs especially suited for camp life.
5. Be a person with taste and the tact to bring musical events to life without offending or being patronizing.
6. Be a person with an obvious, overt excitement about music.
7. Be a person with resourcefulness in order to utilize limited materials to their best advantages.

8. Be a person with organizational ability in order to organize camp shows, talent evenings, and amateur contests with dispatch and meaning.
9. Be a person able to guide campers in making simple, interesting musical instruments.
10. Be a person with the ability to attract the campers toward a natural acceptance of music as a vital part of camp life.

MUSICAL ACTIVITIES WITHIN THE CAMP PROGRAM

Throughout the day from reveille to taps, many opportunities unfold in which music adds immeasurably to camp enjoyment. Camp life is a self-contained environment and music is ideal in such a setting. The following are occasions in which music can enhance life in camp:

1. *Beginning and Ending the Day.* It is often customary to have some manner of instrumental or vocal salute to the day's beginning. The same is true at the end of the day.
2. *Mealtimes.* A wise leader can inject singing at mealtimes without competing with the physical process of eating. The following illustrate mealtime musical activities: a grace sung before the campers begin eating; a spirited song sung between courses; singing while the campers form a "chow line"; a soloist or small group performs while the others eat; recorded music as a relaxing background during the meal itself; and community singing when the meal is finished.
3. *Campfire Time.* Campfire time is a nostalgic moment in the life of every camper. Songs of sentiment, patriotism, nature, and spirituality can add to the beautiful memories each camper will carry with him throughout his life. An open fire is also an appropriate occasion for persons to perform as soloists. This is also an excellent opportunity for the music counselor to introduce the campers to a new song.
4. *Outdoor Hikes.* There is no better setting for the great songs of the out-of-doors than on a hiking trip. The weary hiker finds strength in singing with others, and the wonders of nature *en route* are given a special flavor by an added song. Rounds and echo songs seem unbelievably beautiful when sung in the hiker's territory.
5. *Spiritual Occasions.* Many camps are under the auspices of various religious denominations. Whether the campers gather in the "Cathedral of the Pines," "The Sabbath Green" or a room designated for spiritual communion, music is ever present. On these occasions the campers' choir of selected voices has an opportunity to share their rehearsed anthem with the others. Here also, is an opportunity for the entire assemblage to sing together.
6. *Just for Fun Around the Piano.* When campers have some free moments it can be expected that one of them will seek a piano in the recreation lodge or mess hall in order to play some familiar song for a group of fellow campers. These informal singing times can be the most popular part of the campers' life. These occasions should be honestly and enthusiastically nurtured by those in charge.
7. *Rest Periods.* Recorded, quiet, instrumental music helps create an atmosphere of relaxation during scheduled rest periods. It may be played through a public address system for the benefit of the entire camp, or on individual tape or disc recorders in various rest areas around the camp.
8. *Talent Shows.* Camp life should be full of occasions in which individuals may express themselves. A musical talent show is a "natural" for this purpose. At these functions campers can sing, play, or dance for the entertainment of the entire camp. Special awards and prizes can be given to campers whose performance captivates the audience. Such recognition and the benefits that derive cannot be overlooked in camp life.
9. *Special Musical Concerts.* One of the great rewards of camp life is sharing in a produc-

tion requiring many hours of planning, work, and rehearsal. These are special performances and are most successful when correlated with all of the other musical events of the camp. In other words, special events should not absorb all of the musical outlets in a camp to the exclusion of more widespread musical experiences. An aware music counselor knows which campers have special talent and the desire to perform. Using these performers and working at specified times during the day, a performance can be presented without undue interference with the regular program. Such performances could include an original operetta or dramatic musical, a concert by a camp band or chorus, and many types of solo performances. Here, too, is an excellent showcase for campers who have been involved with modern dance.

In addition to the above, music offers the world of camping many rewarding opportunities and experiences. An outline of these are given below.

Singing in camp should include:

1. Simple novelty songs
2. Folk songs
3. Nature songs
4. Rounds
5. Serious songs
6. Heritage songs
7. Hymns and spiritual songs
8. Popular songs

Playing in camp should include:

1. Harmonicas
2. Ukuleles
3. Guitars
4. Simple percussion instruments (drums, sticks, woodblocks, etc.)
5. Autoharps
6. Pianos (where practical)
7. Easy-to-carry instruments (trumpet, violin)

Dancing in camp should include:

1. Folk dancing
2. Square dancing
3. Modern interpretive dancing
4. Popular dancing

Listening in camp should include:

1. Recordings of popular music
2. Recordings of serious music
3. Music brought into camp via radio and TV

SELECTED REFERENCES

ALBRIGHT, JOE NED. *The Administration of Summer Music Programs in School Systems in the United States.* Unpublished doctoral dissertation, Columbia University, 1963.

CHEYETTE, IRVING. *Songs for Camp and Campus.* Westbury, L. I.: Pro Art Publishing Co., 1960.

EGBERT, MARION. "Music Is What's Happening." *Parks and Recreation.* (June, 1970):22-24, 57-60.

JOSEPH, JAMES. *Careers Outdoors.* rev. ed. New York: Nelson Pub., 1969.

Music Is Recreation. New York: National Recreation Association, 1961.

Social Recreation Leadership. Delaware, Ohio: Cooperative Recreation Service, Inc., 1927.

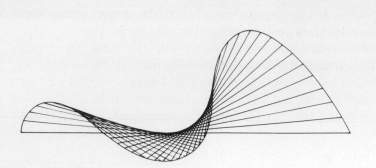

3.

music in industry

Despite almost universal belief to the contrary, gratification, ease, comfort, diversion and a state of having achieved all one's goals do not constitute happiness for man. We are coming to a conception of happiness that differs fundamentally from the storybook version.

John W. Gardner

Music in industrial recreation fills many important needs. It serves as a participatory outlet for amateur music-making and also promotes public relations through performance. Several large industrial firms give evidence of first-rate, and even large scale, music programs for their employees.

Beside the requisite of strong management support, the enthusiasm of a good music director is perhaps the most important single factor for success. Several companies report that the ebb and tide of a good program reflects directly on the person in charge of its organization. Company-sponsored music offerings consist chiefly of choruses, bands, orchestras, and folk dance groups. These allow for maximum involvement and seem to be the most popular with employees. Getting such groups started requires optimum organization and planning. In the beginning stages, facilities and equipment are important. The following are recommendations of the National Industrial Recreation Association.

FACILITIES AND EQUIPMENT REQUIREMENTS OF A BEGINNING EMPLOYEE MUSIC GROUP

The first question often asked when a new employee recreation activity is proposed is how much is it going to cost, or what is it going to require in the way of equipment.[1] Below are recommended facilities and equipment for starting and running an employee music group. Not all items are absolutely essential, of course.

1. *Rehearsal Room.* Whether it be a band, orchestra, or chorus, a rehearsal room of some kind is essential. Ideally, it should be a spacious room with good lighting—a room that is acoustically treated, and one that has controllable temperature for both summer and winter. If the company has no space, perhaps arrangements can be made for one of the music rooms of the public schools, or for space in some other nearby building.

---

1. Taken from *Recreation Management* (March, 1965):27. Used by permission of the National Industrial Recreation Association, Chicago.

2. *Risers.* Though not necessary at the outset, risers are a desirable goal. For the band or orchestra, the semicircular staging should be about four feet wide, each tier being about six inches above the other. For greatest economy, the risers should be in movable sections so that they can be transported from the rehearsal room to the concert location.

3. *Podium.* Whether or not the instrumental and vocal groups are on risers, the conductor must have a podium so that he is raised above the performers and can be seen. A portable platform four feet square that is solidly built is adequate. Of course, podiums can be circular in shape, or made in any design.

4. *Chairs.* The chairs can be of the folding variety and these are widely used. It is best, however, to have chairs that help the performers sit in a good playing posture. Many companies make chairs specifically designed for instrumental and vocal performers.

5. *Music Stands.* Music stands may be either the player's responsibility, or a part of the organization's permanent equipment. The folding stands are adequate, but it is much more satisfactory to have professional stage stands with wide shelves. They are solidly built and can be easily adjusted for good vision. Their appearance, too, is much nicer.

6. *Music Files.* It goes without saying that the groups must have sheet music. Building a music library is a gradual and somewhat expensive investment. The expense of music justifies the purchase of files that will make it possible to keep the music in order and in good condition. Sheet music is usually eight and one-half by eleven inches, so that regular office files suffice. Of course, band marches are written so that they may be placed on instrument lyres for marching. If you have a marching band, you will eventually want file drawers to accommodate the smaller sheet music.

7. *Sorting Shelves.* Obviously not an essential item, the sorting rack is an important facility. It is like a bookshelf in appearance with the exception that the shelves are at a music stand angle for the purpose of sorting music for filing or distribution. After a concert, for example, the music must be taken from the individual players and filed. If each selection can be spread out on the rack, the music can quickly be accumulated in proper order. Likewise before a performance, a new selection can be quickly laid out and accumulated for each player's folder.

8. *Mending Machine.* You should have a supply of clear tape for mending tears in the music. There are edging machines available, too, that will enable you to put an edge of plastic tape around the music to protect it from tearing. The machine is not expensive and the music lasts much longer with this kind of protection.

9. *Music Folders.* Each player needs a folder for the music that is currently being rehearsed. Plain manila folders are sufficient. Some music stores have very fine folders available free of charge as a service to local music groups.

10. *Instruments.* Most instruments should be owned by the individual players. It is not unusual, however, that an organization own the Sousaphones, tympani, bass drum, parade drums, and cymbals. In some instances, they may own bassoons, oboes, English horns and French horns. Wherever possible, it's best if the instruments are owned by the players.

11. *Instrument Storage.* Anything as expensive as instruments must be well cared for. They should not only be in cases, but there should be a good storage location where the temperature is even, and they may be safe from fire, water, and theft. Such lockers can be built by anyone who is good at cabinet making.

12. *Uniforms.* Band uniforms, tuxedos for the orchestra, or choir robes should probably be the last item purchased for an employee music group. It is important that the group first prove itself in performance. There is nothing that looks so ridiculous as a beautifully outfitted group that performs badly.

Good uniforms require dust- and moth-proof closeting. If the closet can be lined with cedar and tightly sealed from dust, the uniforms will last much longer. Again a handy company carpenter could build this equipment without much expense.

Music facilities may be as elaborate or as modest as one can afford. It is good economy, however, to provide protection and proper storage facilities for the instruments and wardrobe, since replacement and maintenance costs can be high.

Besides traditional performance in large group ensembles, the recreation program for employees is enriched by such activities as Christmas shows, variety shows, operettas, participation in civic parades, and festivals or pageants. Within all of these activities, there are outlets for every kind of musical taste (from rock to the classics), and for all kinds of musical combinations. For instance, there are barbershop quartets, choraleers, jazz combos, string quartets, drum and bugle corps, and even bagpipers.

Persons of varying ages can participate together. Both athletes and the nonathletes can join in any type of musical activity. But, most important of all, is the fellowship among employees and administrators in all company departments that usually result from making music.

The following is a partial list of companies and business establishments that have been known for their sponsorship of music programs. Such sponsorship reflects an interest in music on the part of industry.

American Telephone & Telegraph
Argonne National Labs
Battelle Memorial Inst.
Boeing Company
Chase Manhattan Club
Continental Steel Corp.
Dominion Foundries & Steel
R. R. Donnelly's & Sons
Eastman Kodak
Ford Motor
General Electric
Goodyear Tire & Rubber

S. C. Johnson & Son
Eli Lilly & Co.
Lockheed
McDonald-Douglass
Monsanto Research
Nationwide Insurance
North American Rockwell
Owens-Illinois
Prudential Insurance
Rochester Gas & Electric
Salt River Project
Westinghouse Air Brake Co.
Longines

SELECTED REFERENCES

"A New Look at Industrial Music." *Recreation Management*, (August, 1964):10-11.
"Employee Music Groups: A Growing Trend." *Recreation Management*, (August, 1969):4-6.
"Facilities and Equipment Requirements of a Beginning Employee Music Group." *Recreation Management*, (March, 1965).
"Industrial Music is Excellent Use for Employees' New Found Leisure," *Recreation Management*, (October, 1964):10-11.
EGBERT, MARION. "Music Is What's Happening." *Parks and Recreation*, (June, 1970):22-24, 57-60.

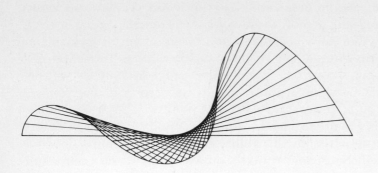

4.

music
for senior
citizens

Whether seventy or seventeen,
There is in every human heart
The lure of wonder, the undaunted challenge of event,
*   and the joy of the game of living.*
We are as young as our faith,
As old as our doubt,
As young as our hope,
As old as our despair.

Samuel Ellman

Interest in the well-being of senior citizens has risen sharply in the past few years. The retirement years are lengthening and expanding as far as age is concerned. People are living longer and retiring earlier. Life expectancy is about seventy-three years and will probably continue to increase. In 1940 there were nine million older Americans; in 1966 there were twenty million. More services and programs of all types are needed. Among them should be activities of a recreational nature to enrich the leisure time typical of these retirement years.

Centers are springing up all over the country to provide the necessary leadership for work with senior citizens. These range from local church groups to municipal Golden Age Clubs. There are also senior citizen housing developments of the commercial type. All of these groups provide recreational programs.

Much of the impetus for the spread of interest in senior citizens was provided by the first White House Conference on the Aging held in 1961. The conference brought together more than 2500 delegates and produced documents relative to all phases of aging. Among these was the "Report on Free Time Activities" which issued several pertinent recommendations excerpted below.

1. Appropriate agencies should be established at federal, state, and local levels to effect cooperative planning, development, and coordination of services of public and private agencies which pertain to recreation for older people.
2. Emphasis be placed upon the urgent need for education of attitudes at every age toward the importance of active and meaningful use of leisure.
3. Existing public and private areas and facilities be made more available for the leisure activities of the aged; and that the special needs of the aged be considered in the planning and construction of all future private and public areas and facilities for recreation.[1]

1. Taken from "Report on Free Time Activities—Recreation, Voluntary Services and Citizenship Participation," Series Number 6, *White House Conference on the Aging* (Washington, D. C.: U. S. Government Printing Office, 1961).

Music naturally becomes a part of every good recreation program for senior citizens. Music has an appeal which can fill many hours of a retired person's life. This is especially true of music which is familiar. The "good old favorites" are always currently popular among older persons. They enjoy musical activities in which they are actively involved as in piano playing, group lessons on musical instruments, group singing, and various instrumental ensembles. Senior citizens also enjoy listening to music for pleasure and relaxation as well as study. All of these music activities should be voluntary and should never overwhelm persons with little musical background or ability.

As with many other recreational programs, the leader must exemplify a sense of informality and an ability to adjust musical activities to the ability level of the group. In work with senior citizens, the ability levels will be widely varied. Some persons reach their older years having had advanced training in music. Others have had little exposure to any type of music. Musical interests will also be different. Some will be enthusiastic about all kinds of music and will enter into any offering of a musical nature. Others will need encouragement for minimum participation.

Many centers for older people have a music club for those who enjoy listening to serious music. Discussion groups develop from this activity and individuals may even do research in the library on musical topics of their choice. Club members may also present musical activities of a performing nature. For example, the music club of the Guy Mason Adult Recreation Center in Washington, D. C., holds a Senior Citizens Festival every year in May. All senior citizens clubs in the area are invited to participate. Various clubs stage skits, musical numbers, dances, and readings. Participants practice many hours before the performances and render with gusto many musical numbers.

Upon reflection, it can easily be seen that music programs for senior citizens could encompass practically every phase of musical activity. Investigation reveals that the ingredients of success in any music project for older persons is leadership and imagination. The following list of ideas are based upon the experiences of music programs for senior citizens in random communities across the nation. They should help lend support to those wishing to carry on musical activities in their own particular locale.

1. Singing in choral groups is a favorite activity, especially for those who have been church choir or community chorus members and have had to "retire" from this activity due to immobility or confinement.

2. Community singing of an informal type can be successful provided the leader is capable of producing a relaxed atmosphere. This is especially pleasant on special days, holidays, etc.

3. Group musical instruction on such instruments as piano, organ, or guitar, is an excellent medium for musical involvement. Local music educators are often helpful in planning and teaching. Civic groups or local clubs are sometimes willing to support this activity. These lessons must always be satisfying and should not be so demanding that they frustrate the learner with an overabundance of skills and knowledge too hurriedly presented.

4. Illustrated lectures of a musical nature are sometimes popular, especially in centers where many persons attend local music concerts and events. In larger cities, preconcert lectures about coming musical programs have met with success.

5. Opportunities should be sought by which older persons can themselves contribute to the musical life of their community. Talented persons can often be recruited as volunteers in situations other than those involving senior citizens.

6. Library books about music and musicians are usually of interest to older persons who may, for the first time in many years, have the time to pursue subjects they have always

wanted to learn. Music is often one of these. A part of the library collection should also include recordings for listening purposes.

7. The socio-cultural background of the group should be the key to many interesting types of programs and activities. Ethnic music, particularly folk songs and dances will often provide the springboard for many persons to participate. Ethnic heritage tends to take on increasing importance in older years. Cultural roots are aptly reflected in the musical character of a group of people.

8. No single activity should overbalance the program. Individual and group experiences should be in balance as should the nature or the activities themselves.

9. Programs of fun and entertainment should be appropriate to adult behavior which can be entered into with enjoyment while maintaining an older person's sense of dignity.

10. Senior citizens often have hidden or obscured talents. These can be tactfully revealed without embarrassment. Encouragement and opportunity are the key ideas in dealing with talented persons who may be shy or self-conscious.

In general, programs for senior citizens in music should also reflect current technological advances. These consist of electronic teaching centers for piano, organ, and guitar. Special instructional materials are provided for group or individual programmed learning on instruments such as these. Technology has now refined the use of transistor equipment, thus enabling persons who want to listen to music to use a compact, portable cassette tape playback set with earphones while still enjoying the presence of a group—some of whom may be watching TV, sewing, etc. The future holds the promise of even more convenient and inexpensive ways to enjoy musical activities.

Somehow, the leisure time of the older years must be filled with positive, enriching experiences if we are to maintain the credibility of a nation growing in civilized and cultural awareness.

SELECTED REFERENCES

BUCKLEY, JOSEPH C. *The Retirement Handbook*. New York: Harper and Brothers, 1953.

CAGAN, MAXWELL S. *There's Gold in Your Golden Age*. Minneapolis: T. S. Denison Co., Inc., 1963.

CARLSON, ADELLE. *Songs to See and Sing*. Nashville, Tenn.: Broadman Press, 1971.

CARNEGIE, DALE. *How to Stop Worrying and Start Living*. New York: Simon and Schuster, 1944-49.

CARNEGIE, DOROTHY. *Don't Grow Old—Grow Up*. New York: E. P. Dutton and Co., Inc., 1959.

HEDGES, SID G. *Fun for the Not So Young*. New York: Philosophical Library, n.d.

KLEEMEIER, ROBERT W. *Aging and Leisure*. New York: Oxford Univ. Press, 1961.

KUBIE, SUSAN H. *Group Work with the Aged*. New York: Gertrude Landau International University Press, 1953.

MADOW, PAULINE. *Recreation in America*. New York: H. W. Wilson Co., 1965.

MATHIASEN, GENEVA. *Criteria for Retirement*. New York: Putnam's Sons, n.d.

MAXWELL, JEAN M. *Centers for Older People*. New York: National Council on Aging, 1962.

MULAC, MARGARET. *Leisure-Time for Living and Retirement*. New York: Harper and Brothers, 1961.

McKINNEY, ANDERSON. *Discovering Music*. New York: The American Book Co., 1949-52.

McMASTER, JENNIE. *New Ideas in Retirement Homes*. Senior Citizen; Vol. XI #2, Feb. 1965, Washington, D. C.

————. *Church Homes with New Features*. Senior Citizen. Vol. XI #4, April 1965, Washington, D. C.

OSTROW, ALBERT. *Fun After Fifty*. New York: Woman's Press, 1953.

SALMON, IRVIN. *Retire and Be Happy*. New York: Greenberg Pub., n.d.

STAFFORD, VIRGINIA, and EISENBURG, LARRY. *Fun for Older Adults*. Nashville, Tenn., Parthenon Press, 1956.

WEINSTOCK, HERBERT. *What Music Is*. New York: Doubleday, 1953 & 66.

WILLIAMS, ARTHUR. *Recreation for the Aging*. New York: Association Press, 1953.

HANDBOOKS AND BULLETINS

Creative Activities. A Manual for Organization Activities for Older People. Division on Welfare of the Aged, Welfare, and Health Council of New York City, 1955.

Education for Later Maturity: A Handbook. William Morrow and Co., Inc., 1955.

Institute of Lifetime Learning. Box 292, Long Beach, California 90801.

Recreation for Later Maturity, March 1956 Bulletin No. 18, North Carolina Recreation Commission, 1956.

Recreation for Older Adults, by Adelle Carlson. Church Recreation Service, Baptist Sunday School Board, Nashville, Tenn., n.d.

Recreation for Senior Citizens, A Report of the Third Southern Regional Institute on Recreation for the Aging. "Retirement—A New Way of Life," by Eugene Friedman, Ph. D., University Extension Division, Univ. of Wisconsin, Madison, Wis.

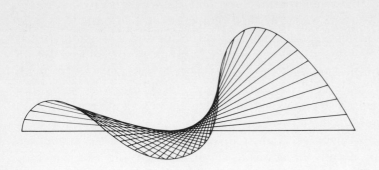

5.

music
in correctional
institutions

He drew a circle that shut me out,
Heretic, rebel, A thing to flout;
But love and I had wit to win,
We drew a circle that took him in.
                                  Edwin Markham

In modern, enlightened institutions, music has been justified as a rehabilitating agent and also as entertainment. This reflects an attitude on the part of prison officials who are looking for new ways to affect behavior changes. In this context, a comprehensive view of recreation which includes music is receiving increasing attention. Evidence of this is appearing in the literature on correction. One illustration is the following statement taken from the latest edition of the well-known book, *The Sociology of Punishment and Correction* by Johnston, Savitz, and Wolfgang: "Early prison reformers hoped that unpleasantness, hard work, solitude, and education would reform men. Contemporary penologists, however, are increasingly aware how difficult it is to affect permanent changes . . . within a prison setting, and . . . are more willing to experiment with new techniques."[1] The authors go on to suggest group and social activities. Music could be a part of many of these.

Music involves many facets of group and individual response. When specifically applied to the needs of persons under correction, these responses can be very positive. The following is a partial list of benefits to be derived from musical participation.

1. Can be effective in evoking interest for some inmates when other means fail.
2. Offers relief from the feelings of confinement.
3. Can become a nonverbal means for anxiety reduction and the release of frustration.
4. Group music-making can provide a sense of belonging and help to alleviate feelings of isolation.
5. Can fill many dull hours, especially for persons with long sentences.
6. Help to reduce feelings of listlessness that sometimes result from serving time.
7. Practice and achievement in instrument playing helps to build morale and self-worth in the accomplishment of a task that continues in difficulty as well as satisfaction.

The character and expressive power of music enable persons of all ages and backgrounds to derive value from either listening or being actively involved in music-making experiences. Music consists of a wide variety of styles—from hillbilly to the classics. It can also be experienced in diverse ways, ranging from simple folk guitar playing to orchestral performance.

1. Norman Johnston, Leonard Savitz, and Marvin Wolfgang, *The Sociology of Punishment and Correction* (New York: John Wiley, 1970), p. 497.

Many large correctional institutions have incorporated musical activities into their recreational programs. In a 1965 survey of twenty prisons, nine had bands, seven had orchestras, and six had choirs or glee clubs. All of the prisons reported musical activities and events on special days or as a part of religious services. While trained recreational directors were hired by all institutions, ten had full or part-time professionals in music. In several instances, prisons allowed talented and trained inmates to guide or direct musical events. These were generally reported to be superbly handled, especially on the part of instrumentalists who were often skilled performers upon prison entrance.[2]

In addition to hired professionals and inmates, many correctional institutions encourage talent from outside the institution. This usually functions as entertainment and is a welcome source of recreation for many inmates. The planning and scheduling of such events is a major responsibility of the recreation director. The following guidelines may help in terms of organization.

1. Musical events should reflect a variety of types and styles.
2. Events should be well publicized among the entire institutional population. A special point should be made to inform those who have special interests or skills related to the coming event.
3. Music events should reflect the totality of psychological experience including the dramatic and sentimental as well as the humorous and heroic.
4. Musical events should not be scheduled when sports activities would be in conflict.
5. Provide visiting performers with suggestions based upon past successful programs.
6. Record performances for use at a later time.

It must be emphasized that the problems and institutional needs relative to correction are complex and multiple. There are many types of institutions ranging from juvenile training centers to federal prisons. In this regard generalizations are difficult to make. In some instances a music program of an educational type can be of value in rehabilitation. In other instances music will consist chiefly of entertainment during recreation periods only. According to the American Correctional Association, the ideal attempt is to keep a balanced program of work, training, and recreation in the day-to-day life of a correctional institution. Taking this view, music can become a reward and reinforcement for work and training.

Music can also stand alone as a constructive source for rehabilitation. It can become a means for use of leisure and recreation. In many training centers for young people, for example, musical events (and even instruction) take on the aspects of typical school music programs in public schools. Supervised athletics, plays, pageants, folk dancing, and musical festivals are among the sponsored events in such institutions.

Regardless of the setting in which it becomes a part, music will serve many valuable functions of institutional correction. In general it can help to bridge many difficulties that arise from confinement and isolation.

SELECTED REFERENCES

American Correctional Association. *Proceedings, 1969 Annual Congress of Correctional Associations*. Washington, D. C.: ACA, 1970.

Creasey, Donald R. *The Prison*. New York: Holt, Rinehart and Winston, Inc., 1961.

Johnston, Norman; Savitz, Leonard; and Wolfgang, Marvin. 2nd ed., *The Sociology of Punishment and Correction*. New York: John Wiley, 1970.

2. Student Research Team, George Waldie, Chairman, Departments of Recreation and Music, University of New Mexico, 1965.

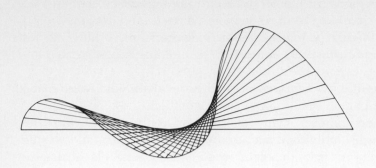

6.

music
in the armed
services

The bow cannot possibly always stand bent, nor can human nature or human frailty subsist without some recreation.

Cervantes

Musical activities can be among the richest offerings of any recreational program for the armed services. All soldiers can participate as either listeners or performers. For example, during one year at Fort Sam Houston, the attendance for the Fourth Army Entertainment Program alone was 772,121. This would be doubled with the inclusion of service club musical and entertainment activities.[1]

To illustrate the widespread nature of music related activities, one has only to read the Army regulation for the administration of facilities and personnel assigned to entertainment-related programs. The text of this regulation follows.

Section I. General

1. *Mission.* The mission of the Army entertainment program is to assist in developing the efficiency and morale of military personnel through cultural, vocational, avocational, creative and/or recreational pursuits by planning, promoting, and developing theatrical and musical activities as an effective means of providing adult special interest outlets in all phases of the performing and tributary arts.

2. *Scope.* The Army entertainment program includes within its functional scope three subprograms of activity: music, theater, and touring shows. Each subprogram is of equal importance in the accomplishment of the mission of the program, is closely allied, and generally interrelated in the development of the overall program. Figures 1, 2, and 3 indicate the sources of touring shows and the activities of the music and theater programs.

   a. Touring shows. Live (professional or amateur, civilian or military, theatrical or musical attractions produced elsewhere and brought to an installation to perform in facilities other than clubs and messes.

   b. Music. All organized music including vocal, instrumental, technical, and listening music activities, except authorized TOE Army bands.

      (1) Vocal activities. Activities which include individual and group recital and concert forms; individual and group folk, popular, country and western, jazz, patriotic

1. Taken from a returned questionnaire completed by the Staff Service Club Director, Fort Sam Houston, Texas, 1968.

and/or military, religious, semiclassical, and classical forms, as well as other types of choral and ensembles (singing in unison or in harmonic parts), both large and small including quintets, quartets, trios, and duos, contests and festivals; choral workshops and/or clinics; singing platoons, singing-on-the-march, and song fests of all types. Solo and group forms may include instrumental accompaniment or be performed a capella, as appropriate.

(2) Instrumental activities. Activities which include the development, maintenance, and use of show and dance bands; small instrumental combinations; individuals and groups specifically developed for use in musical theater activities; individual and group recital and concert forms; individual and group popular, country and western, rhythm and blues, rock and roll, jazz, dixieland, semiclassical, and classical forms; musical ensembles of all types; symphonic, orchestral, chamber, and band groups, as well as all types of solo performances; contests and festivals; solo and group practice sessions; music fairs, and music workshops and clinics.

(3) Technical music activities. Activities which include musical direction; composition and/or creative writing; theory and harmony; arranging and orchestration; music copying; music management; interpretation of musical styles; lyric writing; accoustics; rehearsal and performance techniques of all types; and care and maintenance of all types of musical equipment.

(4) Listening activities. A series of carefully planned and produced listening programs including all types of recorded music; live performances by musical artists (both vocal and instrumental), lecturers, critics, and teachers; music education and appreciation activities; demonstrations and clinics by all types of musical and educational organizations and/or individuals. Emphasis is placed on carefully annotated programs emphasizing high performance standards whether program is performed live or recorded.

c. Theater. All organized theatrical activity including dramatic musical-theater, technical, and listening programs.

(1) Dramatic activities. Activities which encourage the development of spoken art forms to include plays of all types (tragedy, comedy, farce, melodrama, and all other types); individual dramatic readings and/or monologs; sketches, skits, and blackouts; large and small dramatic groups; play-reading groups; choral speech or reading groups; little theater groups; dramatic workshops and clinics; drama contests and festivals; radio and television workshops and productions.

(2) Musical-theater activities. Activities which include musical comedies, musical dramas, musical revues, operas, operettas, thematic productions of all types; variety shows; band shows; dance productions of all types; contests and festivals; all other forms of musical theater whether performed individually or by a group.

(3) Technical theater activities. Activities which include theatrical direction; playwriting; and other forms of creative writing; lighting design and implementation; scenic and costume design and construction; makeup; stage management; oral interpretation, play production; choreography; dance production; techniques of announcing; technical production; sound reproduction; rehearsal and performance techniques of all types; and care and maintenance of all types of theatrical equipment.

(4) Listening activities. A series of carefully planned and produced listening programs including all forms of theatrical materials; live performances by theatrical artists, lecturers, critics, and teachers; demonstrations and clinics by all types of theatrical and educational organizations and/or individuals. Emphasis is placed on carefully

annotated programs emphasizing high performance standards whether a program is performed live or recorded.[2]

As a morale factor, music has been recognized since the Fife and Bugle Corps during the Revolutionary War. The military band has been integral to the armed forces since the Civil War and singing was widely encouraged during the First World War—as witnessed by the many well-loved songs of that period.

Recreation specialists in music with the Armed Forces Special Services often come from career employees. Aside from their status, however, these specialists are required to have the Baccalaureate Degree in vocal or instrumental music plus two years of successful teaching experience directing a variety of musical activities. Experience as an entertainer or performer is non-qualifying.

The day-to-day work of service music personnel can be highly creative. Special Services officers and club directors are constantly challenged to find imaginative ways involving service men in musical groups and performances. Variety shows are among the most popular ways. Most service clubs schedule these regularly. The following schedule is typical. The music and dance events are underlined.

MAY 1970

SUNDAY	MONDAY	TUESDAY	WEDNESDAY	THURSDAY	FRIDAY	SATURDAY
1000 Morning Music 1300 Jam Session 1500 Ping Pong Contest 2000 Soldier Show						1000 Record Requests 1300 Art Corner 1900 May Bingo 1915 The Whitman Dancers Show
1000 Morning Music 1300 Combo Time 2000 Soldiers Entertain	1900 Ceramics Class 2000 Leathercraft Class	1900 Classical Record Requests 2000 "May" Dance	1900 Classical Record Requests 2000 Gameroom Contests	1900 "Life and Yahtze" Games 2000 Movies Refreshments	2030 "Pioneer" Dance	1000 Record Requests 1300 Art Corner 1500 Bridge Games 1900 Record Roulette 2045 Soldier Show
1000 Morning Music 1300 Club Combo 2000 Soldier Show	1900 Ceramics Class 2000 Leathercraft Class	1900 Classical Record Requests 2000 "Spring is Here" Dance	1900 Pokend Games 2000 Pool, Ping Pong Contests	1900 Concentration 2000 Movies Refreshments	1900 Chuck-a-luck Games 2000 "You can Use It" Bingo	1000 Record Request 1300 Art Corner 1500 Bridge Games 1900 Combo Rehearsal 1915 Starlit Revue Show

Continued on page 22.

2. Issued by U. S. Army, Regulation AR 28-13, TAGO 7841.

MAY 1970

SUNDAY	MONDAY	TUESDAY	WEDNESDAY	THURSDAY	FRIDAY	SATURDAY
1000 Morning Music 1300 Guitars and Songs 2000 Visiting Combo	1900 Ceramics Class 2000 Leathercraft Class	1900 Dance Class 2000 "Ballroom" Dance	1900 Soldier Birthday Party 2000 Gameroom Contests	1900 Two for the Money	1900 Company Team Party 2000 "Consequence" Bingo	1000 Record Request 1300 Art Corner 1900 Game-a-rama 2045 Dorothy Inderleid Show
1000 Morning Music 1300 Jam Session 2000 Soldiers Entertain	1900 Ceramics Class 2000 Leathercraft Class	1900 Classical Music Requests 2000 "Spring" Dance	1900 Horse Race Games 2000 Pool, Ping Pong Contests	1900 Bowling 2000 Movies Refreshments	1900 Video Village Game 2000 "Smokers" Bingos	1000 Record Request 1300 Art Corner 1915 Belmont Fun

7.

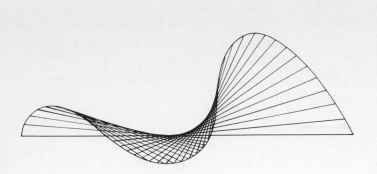

music
on pleasure
cruisers

This much I know when all is done,
That he who's never tasted fun
Will think of life as one grand bore
And shouldn't get to Heaven's door.

John Batcheller

Recreation work aboard ship is probably the most glamorous in the field. It is associated with travel, new sights, interesting people, and the attendant excitement of visiting foreign ports. Because of this, positions for qualified cruise directors or social leaders are very limited. Requirements always include previous experience in resorts, country clubs, or hotels. In addition, most ship lines maintain such requirements as the ability to speak foreign languages, knowledge of the ports to be visited, organizational ability, and most important of all, a pleasant personality with which to encounter various situations and many different kinds of people.

On the larger cruise vessels, music permeates most recreational activities either as a direct participative experience or as a background to an event. Orchestras and dance bands are probably the most common form of musical entertainment. Roving musicians with solo instruments, such as accordion or violin, are becoming more popular. Recorded music is piped into staterooms, and onto game decks and pool areas. Active music participation in passenger choruses and talent shows are effective leisure activities common on mainline cruises.

Additional facilities in which music could have a part include a 10,000 book library on the S. S. France, a 66,000 ton vessel carrying 2044 passengers. A selection of recordings and tapes with earphones could be added to such a ship library. Books about the lives of musicians or the art of music would naturally be of interest to many passengers. For many people, the relaxing atmosphere of cruise travel provides a first opportunity to "take the time" to explore the arts. Busy work routines and the pressure of responsible jobs are left on shore. The leisure time away from the telephone can be filled with rewarding pleasures always thought too time consuming at home.

The theater, used primarily for movies, is also available for talent shows and music productions on board the larger vessels. For example, the MS Sagafjord, on the Norwegian-American Line (21,000 tons) has a 250 seat theater that is used for numerous events and musical programs including travel talks about each port of call. These talks could include local onshore musical events, concerts, and folk festivals which passengers might attend. Such musical events often become memorable highlights of travel cruises and form the basis for cultural understanding.

On many pleasure cruisers, music permeates the events of each day. The following schedule is typical and is taken directly from the "Events du jour" of the S. S. France on their Noel Cruise of 1964. The several events which include music or related activities are in bold.

EVENTS DU JOUR

7:00 A.M.	Breakfast is served
8:00 A.M.	Holy Mass
8:00 A.M.	Calisthenics
9:00 A.M.	Protestant services
10:00 A.M.	Holy Mass
10:00 A.M.	Your lesson in French
10:30 A.M.	Hostess hour
11:00 A.M.	**Free dance lesson**
11:00 A.M.	**Teen-age fun and games**
11:00 A.M.	Clay pigeon shooting
11:30 A.M.	Your morning forum at sea
11:45 A.M.	Aperitif time (Music by René MOOS in the Riviera Lounge)
12:30 P.M.	Luncheon is served
12:30 P.M. TO 2:00 P.M.	Buffet luncheon is served
2:30 P.M.	Duplicate bridge tournament
3:00 P.M.	Informal card games
3:30 P.M.	Shuffleboard tournament begins
4:00 P.M.	Need help with your Apache costume
4:00 P.M.	**Tea and bingo (music by Rene MOOS—St. Tropez Lounge)**

4:15 P.M.	**Recorded concert**
4:30 P.M.	Clay pigeon shooting
4:30 P.M.	Register for children's costume party
5:00 P.M.	Children's costume party
6:15 P.M.	Your late news report
6:30 P.M.	Cocktails are served in all bars **(Music in Riviera Lounge and Left Bank Cafe)**
7:30 P.M.	Dinner is served
9:00 P.M.	**Dance music**
9:30 P.M.	**Music for dancing**
10:00 P.M.	**Ball Apache**
10:00 P.M. TO MIDNIGHT	Young adults swimming party
10:30 P.M.	"Surprise a la Francaise"
11:00 P.M.	Noctambules (night owls)
11:00 P.M.	**Music by Paul Gene Trio**
MIDNIGHT	**Piano magic**
MIDNIGHT TO 1:30 A.M.	Buffet is served

Steamship and pleasure cruise lines are numerous. Each has special activities for passengers according to number of persons aboard, size of ship, ports of call, time of year, etc. Upon inquiry, it was reported that the smaller transport ships, carrying as few as twelve passsengers obviously have no recreation director as such. However, recreational facilities are available in every instance. The following list will serve as a handy reference for anyone interested in investigating recreational programs and facilities relative to pleasure liners.

Alcoa Steamship Co., Inc.; 17 Battery Place; New York, New York 10004.
Alaskan Cruises, Inc.; Department V. J. Vance Building; Seattle, Washington 98103.
American Export Lines; 550 South Flower Street; Los Angeles, California 90017.
American President Lines; Pier 9; Jersey, City, New Jersey 07303.
Atlantic Cruise Line, Inc.; 520 Biscayne Blvd.; Miami, Florida 33101.
Barber Steamship Lines, Inc.; 17 Battery Place, New York, New York 10004.
Belgian Line; 67 Broad Street; New York, New York 10004.
Bergen Steamship Co., Inc.; 576 Fifth Avenue; New York, New York 10036.
Black Diamond Line; 2 Broadway; New York, New York 10004.
Booth Lines; 17 Battery Place; New York, New York 10004.
Cairn-Thompson Line; 315 Saint Sacrament Street; Montreal, Canada.
Canadian Pacific Steamships; Nm. 115 Windsor Station; Montreal, Canada.
Caribbean Cruise Lines; Southern Building; Washington, D. C. 20005.
Chilean Line; American Bank Building; New Orleans, Louisiana 70112.

Christensen Canadian African Lines; 468 Saint John Street; Montreal, Canada.

Circle Lines Sightseeing, Inc.; 303 West Forty-second Street; New York, New York 10036.

Concordia Line; 90 Broad Street; New York, New York 10004.

Cosmopolitan Line; 42 Broadway; New York, New York 10004.

Costa Line; 26 Broadway; New York, New York 10004.

Delta Line; Hibernia Bank Building; New Orleans, Louisiana 70112.

Dorian Cruises; c/o International Tours; Miami Beach, Florida 33101.
   This company includes: Adriatica Line, Chandris Cruises, Epirotiki Lines, Helmes Lines, Nomikos Lines, Typaldos Line.)

East Asiatic Co.; 465 California Street; San Francisco, California 94104.

Farrell Lines; 1740 Book Tower; Detroit, Michigan 48226.

Fred Olsen Line; 465 California Street; San Francisco, California 94104.

French Line; 610 Fifth Avenue; New York, New York 10020.

Furness Lines; 355 Burrard Street; Vancouver, B. C., Canada.

Grace Line, Inc.; 3 Hanover Square; New York, New York 10004.

Gulf & South American Steamship Co., Inc.; American Flag Vessels; P.O. Box 50938; New Orleans, Louisiana 70150.

Hamburg-American Line & North German Lloyd; 140 South Dearborn Street; Chicago, Illinois 60603.

Hamburg-Chicago Line; 468 Saint John Street, Montreal, Canada.

Hansa Line; 120 Wall Street, New York, New York 10005.

Hanseatic-Vaasa Lines; 530 West Sixth Street; Los Angeles, California 90014.

Head Line & Lord Line; P.O. Box Place D'Armes 1086; Coristine Building; Montreal, Canada.

Hellenic Lines Limited; 39 Broadway; New York, New York 10006.

Hoegh Lines; 51 Broad Street; New York, New York 10004.

Holland-American Line; Pier 40; North River New York 12856.

Independent Gulf Line; 442 Canal Street; New Orleans, Louisiana 70130.

Interocean Lines; 310 Sansome Street; San Francisco, California 94104.

Isthmian Lines, Inc.; 90 Broad Street; New York, New York 10004.

Italian Line; Department U-1, 1 Whitehall Street, New York, New York 10004.

Johnson Line; 511 Board of Trade Building; Portland, Oregon 97208.

Knutsen Line; Bakke Steamship Corp.; 141 Battery Street; San Francisco, California 94111.

Lykes Lines; Department 61, Lykes Brothers' Steamship Co., Inc.; New Orleans, Louisiana 70130.

Marine Cooks and Stewards; 675 Fourth Street, Brooklyn, New York 11215.

Matson Lines; 215 Market Street; San Francisco, California 94111.

Moore-McCormack Lines; 2 Broadway; New York, New York 10004.

Nervion Line; 327 Saint Charles Street; New Orleans, Louisiana 70130.

Norwegian American Line; 24 State Street; New York, New York 10004.

Ozean/Stinnes Lines; Box 2277 Custom House Station; New Orleans, Louisiana 70116.

Port Line; 606 South Hill Street; Los Angeles, California 90014.

Rohner, Gehrig Lines; 1 Whitehall Street; New York, New York 10004.

Royal Mail Lines; 1731 Exchange Building; Seattle, Washington 98104.

Saguenay Shipping Limited; 1060 University Street; Montreal, Canada.

Sailors Union of the Pacific; 675 Fourth Avenue, Brooklyn, New York 11215.

Seafarer's International Union of Canada; 289 Main Street; Vancouver, B. C., Canada.

States Lines; 105 West Adams Street; Chicago, Illinois 60603.

Swedish American Line; The White Viking Fleet; 636 Fifth Avenue; New York, New York 10020.

Thordean Lines; 90 Broad Street; New York, New York 10004.

Torm Lines; 85 Broad Street; New York, New York 10004.

Union Castle Line; 581 Fifth Ave.; New York, New York 10017.

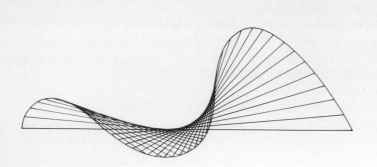

8.

music
in clinical
institutions

Man is, properly speaking, based upon hope; he has no other possession but hope; this world of his is emphatically the place of hope.

Carlyle

The entire field of clinical music is vast and highly specialized. For this reason it is impossible to include a comprehensive program here. However, there are several theoretical and practical suggestions for treatment which could provide an introduction to the field in general. Anyone interested in specializing in clinical music should be prepared to receive considerable training. Primary in this training should be a background in music methods—both general and specific.

Clinical music is the use of music in the education and the treatment of persons needing special help resulting from functional disorders. It is directly involved with both rehabilitation and education. Used clinically, music releases anxieties. Even the smallest accomplishments in mastering a musical activity will build confidence and self-worth. It is expressive and does not require words. Thus music provides a natural means for expressing feelings and moods. Music stimulates the individual as a whole and creates an environment that is noncompetitive and undemanding. It is also appealing and stimulates response.

In addition, musical problems may be approached through the development of skills and concepts. These are essential to the nature of music in terms of its elements, i.e., pitch duration, texture, color, form. These are likewise the results of experiences in listening, singing, playing instruments, moving to music and creating music. Authentic responses of this type can be made in clinical situations regardless of the level of response or the quality of the rendition.

Music can serve to bridge problems with solutions for many persons with emotional or mental disorders. Generally, their problems include tension, fear, depression, defensiveness, and disorganization in thought patterns as well as problems which are the result of physical impairment. Consequently these persons need communication, interaction with others, confidence, and a sense of belonging. They also need to discover avenues that can lead them toward better physical coordination and ways of making legitimate compensations.

For the recreational leader who is involved in clinical music the following are some musical assets which may serve as guidelines.
That music:

1. Can establish communication without verbalization and can also serve to stimulate verbalization when needed.

2. Eliminates the friction that words may produce.
3. Overcomes antagonism, isolation, and nonparticipation.
4. Attracts attention, produces various moods, and stimulates imagery.
5. Offers a variety of skill levels. A person with a low failure factor can experience a feeling of achievement as he masters a simple musical response, such as striking a triangle, beating a drum, or simply tapping his foot.
6. Affords a variety of expressive outlets. For example, emotions can be expressed musically by uncomplicated listening experiences. Here, a person is not required to perform any kind of physical act that might otherwise prove threatening. Improvisation on an instrument often allows emotions to be released or even, in some instances, discovered. The many ways a person can move himself or parts of his body to music can be another expressive outlet.
7. Creates an ideal environment for role-playing. A person can "be" someone or something other than what he is as he sings or moves (dances).
8. Can subtly invite the antisocial person to become increasingly involved with his peers. A socially retarded person, for example, can learn a skill that is accepted in public. Singing, dancing, or playing instruments, for example, can be a step toward group acceptance.
9. Affords a means through which aggressiveness can be lived out.
10. Creates a learning environment that can be noncompetitive. This implies few performance requirements of a strict nature.

Objectives of Clinical Music. The objectives of a clinical music program should reflect the function of music in combination with other avenues of experience, thus fostering the total development of the person. The following statements of primary and secondary objectives illustrate the many possible aspects of a music program and can serve as guides for establishing goals in many other situations. These objectives were developed for use at the Georgia Retardation Center in Atlanta.[1]

CLINICAL MUSIC PROGRAM OBJECTIVES

A. As a result of the Music Program, students at the Georgia Retardation Center will obtain the *Primary Objectives* of personal development that enables the individual to interact as a social being and will therefore:

1. Develop satisfactory social relationships through interaction with peers and adults in the numerous group experiences and environments provided for them.
2. Develop a likeable personality and a proper self-image in an atmosphere of contentment and acceptance offered in the musical setting, with opportunities for pleasurable, successful achievement building self-confidence and determination.
3. Develop an appreciation of the arts and desire and ability to express oneself creatively through various media.
4. Develop skill and the desire to be both participant and spectator in worthwhile leisure-time activities: sports, music, circus, parties, church, etc., both on campus and in the community.
5. Develop an awareness of the spiritual aspects of life through music.
6. Develop responsive vocalization and spontaneous expression through the musical stimuli in order to foster verbalization.

1. Taken from "The Role of the Clinical Music Program in an Inter-Disciplinary Setting," Clinical Music Program, Donna Cypret, Director, Georgia Retardation Center, 1970. Used by permission.

7. Develop auditory discrimination and memory; learning many speech sounds, increasing vocabulary and rote learning.
8. Develop meaningful associations of spoken words with pictures, objects, people, action, direction, moving from the familiar to the new.
9. Develop concepts of shape, size, and relativity; big and little, same or different, near and far, few and lot, long and short, etc., through the use of visual, auditory, and kinesthetic stimuli.
10. Develop control of movement and certain motor skills through the use of instruments and movement to music.
11. Develop concept of relaxation and skilled coordination through musical activities (especially applicable to cerebral palsied students).
12. Develop happier, alert, and better motivated students even when musical growth is small.

B. The *Subsidiary Objectives* of creating a capacity for musical activity:

1. *Appreciation.* Through many experiences in structured musical settings, it is hoped that every student at the Georgia Retardation Center will:

(a) Respond in a sensitive way to the varied moods expressed by the music he hears, moves to, sings, and plays.
(b) Participate in musical activities with enthusiasm, pleasure, and success.
(c) Demonstrate potential for gaining meaning from the musical stimuli "Conceptualization."

2. *Musical competencies.* As a result of the Music Program, some students will:

(a) *Listening*

(1) Be aware of music, both live and recorded.
(2) Respond to timbre of various instruments.
(3) Recognize timbre of various instruments.
(4) Respond to music that is of different styles, i.e., folk, serious, rock, country, sacred, etc.
(5) Recognize music of different styles.
(6) Respond to music of various media, i.e., orchestral, vocal, etc.
(7) Recognize music of various media.
(8) Respond to music of various tonalities, i.e., pentatonic scale, major scale, minor scale, whole-tone scale.
(9) Recognize music of various tonalities.
(10) Respond to basic contrasts in music, i.e., high and low, up and down, fast and slow, soft and loud, even and uneven, sound and silence, long and short.
(11) Recognize basic contrasts in music.

(b) *Singing*

(1) Spontaneously vocalize tonal, rhythmic, or exclamatory sounds to composed songs.
(2) Spontaneously vocalize improvised melodies expressing own feelings.
(3) Spontaneously verbalize improvised melodies expressing own feelings.
(4) Sing melodies or melodic fragments of composed songs in a recognizable manner.
(5) Sing melodies or melodic fragments of composed songs on pitch.

(c) *Playing instruments*

(1) Explore and experiment with various instruments.
(2) Use instruments to play the basic beat of melodies.
(3) Use instruments (with or without assistance) to play the rhythm of the melody or melodic fragments.
(4) Develop a beating pattern which is one of complete rhythmic freedom.

(d) *Moving to music*

(1) Participate freely in action songs and singing games.
(2) Dramatize song through characterization and bodily motion.
(3) Respond to the rhythm of the music by performing with large bodily movement, i.e., walk, run, gallop, skip, jump.
(4) Emphasize beat and rhythmic patterns by using a variety of physical responses, i.e., tap, clap, sway (with or without assistance).

(e) *Creativity*

(1) Spontaneously improvise melodies by singing or playing instruments.
(2) Spontaneously improvise rhythm patterns by singing or playing instruments.
(3) Express the mood of music being sung or played through bodily movement.
(4) Create additional words for songs he knows.
(5) Participate in the creation and performance of musical playlets.

3. *Musical concepts.* As a result of the music program, some students will be able to develop a capacity for musical perception resulting in the formation of musical concepts and will therefore be able to:

(a) *Melody*

(1) Distinguish melodic range as: high, medium, low.
(2) Identify melodic direction in terms of: stepwise, skipwise, jump.

(b) *Rhythm*

(1) Recognize contrasts in sound and silence.
(2) Recognize contrasts in long and short.
(3) Identify overall rhythmic movement as even or uneven.
(4) Recognize short rhythmic phrases as same or different.
(5) Recognize that music moves in groups of 2.
(6) Recognize that music moves in groups of 3.

(c) *Harmony*

(1) Recognize the presence of multiple sounds within a musical entity.
(2) Reflect awareness of multiple sound by singing a melody with contrasting accompaniment.
(3) Reflect awareness of multiple sound by playing a melody with contrasting accompaniment.
(4) Reflect awareness of multiple sounds by playing contrasting patterns as accompaniments to songs by ostinato.
(5) Reflect awareness of multiple sounds by playing contrasting patterns as accompaniments to songs by cluster.
(6) Reflect awareness of multiple sounds by playing contrasting patterns as accompaniments to songs by interval.

(7) Reflect awareness of multiple sounds by playing contrasting patterns as accompaniments to songs by chord.

(d) *Form*

(1) Identify melodic and rhythmic phrases as same or different.
(2) Recognize sections within a compositions as being same or different.
(3) Reflect awareness of phrase in singing.
(4) Demonstrate awareness of same-different phrases by selecting same-different instruments for accompaniment.
(5) Indicate recognition of phrases by responding with appropriate body movements.
(6) Develop contrasting movements appropriate for same-different sections or phrases.
(7) Associate same-different geometric shapes with same-different phrases or sections.

(e) *Expressions*

(1) Recognize contrasts in dynamics—loud and soft.
(2) Recognize contrasts in tempo—fast-slow.
(3) Identify some common orchestral instruments.
(4) Associate instruments with appropriate high-low category.
(5) Learn to associate musical sounds with particular moods when selecting instruments for accompaniments.
(6) Indicate awareness of overall mood in dance movements.
(7) Choose appropriate instruments when adding sound effects to stories and poetry or when creating accompaniments for familiar songs.

Clinical music involves many integrative processes. These contain elements which may be physical, psychological or physiological. For this reason, persons specializing in clinical music as a career should have in-depth training. This is especially important in the areas of psychological functioning.

Many recreational leaders are trained in physical education programs which emphasize motor and physical skills. Such persons are frequently involved in recreation programs which have an adjunct of rehabilitation in terms of muscular and functional development. From that standpoint, it seems appropriate to include in this book a discussion of clinical music as related to the treatment of such problems as mobility, endurance, and coordination. These aspects make up the general area known as functional therapy.

There are multiple uses for music as functional therapy. They are most often reflected in rehabilitation work with muscular-coordinative skills. Among these are to (1) increase mobility, (2) lengthen endurance, and (3) develop coordination.

The term coordination covers a wide area. It includes eye-hand coordination, hand-foot coordination, hand-arm coordination, and so forth. Musical activities can assist in all of these problems. Reciprocal patterns, such as those involved in walking, may also be treated in a functional music program.

The proper concern is to link music with physical-functional conditions as a corrective device. Specific musical instruments can be used to increase mobility or to establish conditions for greater endurance. In fact, with occupational therapy as a foundation. The use of musical instruments is sometimes the essential part of functional therapy. A detailed summary of musical activities directly related to the clinical treatment of mobility, endurance, and coordinative problems may be found in Appendix G, p. 126.

CLINICAL MUSIC FOR THE RETARDED

There is increasing national attention given to retardation. Many agencies, including the schools, are devoting considerable effort in meeting the needs of retarded persons. The goals and objectives of music within retardation programs have been advanced by substantial numbers of music educators. They are found to be of considerable importance in carrying out a successful program. An excellent example of the comprehensiveness of such a set of objectives is easily seen in the quoted portion from the Georgia Retardation Center given on pp. 27-30.

Another excellent statement of objectives and suggested teaching approaches is that prepared by Marjorie Reeves for the schools of Illinois. The primary objective of music as quoted from this publication is "to provide every child the opportunity to experience music and express himself through music to the best of his ability. . . , the key is 'to the best of his ability.' "[2]

Most music programs for retarded persons reflect the philosophy that clinical music involves a learning process coincidental with the needs of retardation. These include a wide range of experiences which imply learning by doing.

A low I.Q. does not hinder a person's need to be creative. In fact, the retarded should be encouraged to discover their own level of expressive creativity. The music specialist must always remember that the quality of the product created is unimportant. The main concern here is spontaneity and freedom. These factors allow expression through various musical activities. Some implications derived from the functional use of music for the retarded follow.

1. Improving recognition of abstract symbols through association of signs with auditory stimuli.
2. Lengthening of ability span through gradually prolonging participation in listening and playing.
3. Developing a wider range of ideas through imagery and dramatization.
4. Enlarging the scope of social interaction by physical response in a group as in folk dancing.
5. Opportunities to "belong" with others in group performing situations.
6. Realization of the similarity of demands among all persons for regulation of behavior in accepted ways since musical experiences can require adherence to a notated score, or to a set of musical principles and aural values.

SUMMARY

One cannot say that music is clinical in itself. It is useful because of the psychological and physiological effects it has on mood and behavior. Used clinically, therefore, music is not an end in itself, but rather a means to treatment. It also enables the person to make better use of other experiences.

Clinical music involves two areas. The first is music itself. This includes music lessons, practice of technique, and the use of certain pieces to produce various responses. The second is the relationship developed between the instructor and patient. Using the flexible medium of his special field, the instructor is an effective therapeutic agent. The atmosphere which he creates, and the relationship he establishes, makes music an activity in the clinical sense.

2. Marjorie Reeves, *Music for Handicapped Children* (Springfield, Illinois: Office of Public Instruction, n.d.). Distributed by Instructional Materials Center for Handicapped Children and Youth, 1020 South Spring Street, Springfield, Illinois 63704.

Used clinically, musical experiences can often cause patients to acquire new and lasting interests in the art itself. In other words, it can be enjoyed as a pastime bringing satisfaction and enrichment long after its educational and therapeutic uses are over.

SELECTED REFERENCES

ANTEY, JOHN W. *Sing and Learn.* New York: The John Day Co., 1965.

CANNER, NORMAN, and KLEBANOFF, HARRIET. And a *Time to Dance.* Boston: Beacon Press, 1968.

CARLSON, BERNIECE, and GINGLAND, DAVID. *Recreation for Retarded Teenagers and Young Adults.* Nashville, Tenn.: Abingdon Press, 1968.

COLE, FRANCES. *Music for Children with Special Needs.* Glendale, California: Bowmar Pub., Co., 1965.

The Expressive Arts for Mentally Retarded. National Association for Retarded Children, Inc., New York, 1967.

GINGLAND, DAVID, and STILES, WINIFRED. *Music Activities for Retarded Children.* Nashville, Tenn.: Abingdon Press, 1965.

HUNT, VALERIE V. *Recreation for the Handicapped.* Englewood Cliffs, N. J.: Prentice-Hall, Inc., 1955.

KOLSTOE, OLIVER. *Teaching Educable Mentally Retarded Children.* New York: Holt Pub. Co., 1970.

"Music As Therapy." (Issue) *Music Journal,* November, 1970.

NORDOFF, PAUL, and ROBBINS, C. *Music Therapy for Handicapped Children.* New York: Rudolf Steiner Pub., 1965.

ROBINS, FERRIS, and ROBINS, JENNET. *Educational Rhythmics for Mentally and Physically Handicapped Children.* New York: Association Press, 1967.

SCHATTNER, REGINA. *Creative Dramatics for Handicapped.* New York: The John Day Co., 1967.

RECORDINGS:

Songs for Children with Special Needs by Frances Cole. Bowmar Records, Inc., Glendale, California.

II.

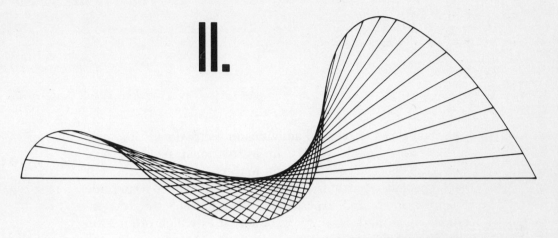

**instructional
ideas and
resources**

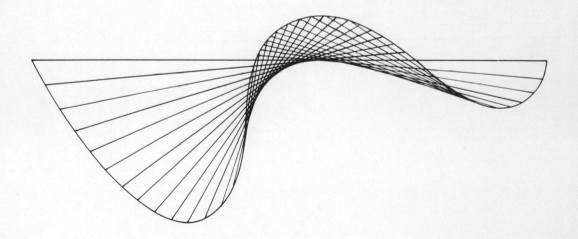

The types of musical activities in recreational programs reflect considerable variety in instructional needs, procedures, levels of accomplishment, and material resources. For each specialized area, there are published sources to provide teaching ideas and experiences. This part of the text includes illustrated descriptions of activities which often form the basis for music programs in such areas as parks and camps. They are organized under the following headings: (1) group singing and song leadership, (2) instrumental accompaniment, (3) sound exploration and choral speaking, and (4) dramatic movement and traditional dancing.

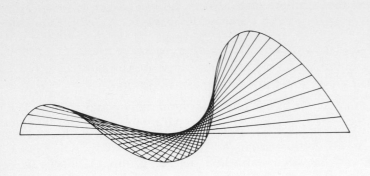

9.

group singing and song leadership

Probably the most rewarding musical experience within a recreational setting is group singing.[1] It provides a music-making experience for persons of all ages and abilities. And, because there is no audience as such, individuals usually become involved without embarrassment or self-consciousness.

The most important single person in any group singing activity is the song leader. His functions are directly related to the needs, interests, and musical capabilities of the group. These may range from indoor auditorium song fests to outdoor camp sings.

The musical abilities within groups will reflect considerable diversity. In some groups, many persons may be able to harmonize by ear or read music with fluency. In others, even a single melody line may be difficult to learn well. For this reason, the song leader must be flexible enough to handle the limitations and aspirations in each group as he finds them.

LEARNING NEW SONGS

Besides learning songs with a book or other visual aid, there will be times when leaders will want to teach new songs by imitation (rote). In fact, recreational singing often requires rote approaches.

The particular style and form of the song determines the nature of the teaching approach. Also, it is good to use a variety of plans to maintain interest. Any one or combination of the following suggestions may be useful depending on the type of song being presented.

1. Leader sings the entire song. Some textual or musical aspect is discussed or pointed out.
2. Leader sings the song phrase by phrase and the group repeats without breaking the rhythm.
3. Group responds on a repeated section that is simple and easily remembered.
4. Group taps or claps the rhythm of the words as the leader repeats the song.
5. Group hums along on the tune before learning words or new verses.
6. Group responds to all or parts of the song with instruments.
7. Group follows musical phrases to recall which are alike and which are different.
8. Group learns by imitation from a recording.

1. An excellent source on singing, which also includes many good recreation songs in notation, is Forrest J. Baird, *Music Skills for Recreation Leaders* (Dubuque, Iowa: William C. Brown Company Publishers, 1963). The authors highly recommend this book to all persons in recreation.

When using any of the approaches above, there are always additional considerations which contribute to the enjoyment and success of the community singing.

1. The song leader should be very familiar with all of the songs to be presented. These should reflect variety and follow thoughtful organization in terms of the singing order. The interests and enjoyment of the group are the primary considerations.

2. A successful leader should project enthusiasm by his physical countenance and the clarity of his conducting. He should be able to use the conventional techniques and know when each is appropriate.

3. The starting pitch of each song should be well established for the group. A chord giving the tonality (key of the song) can be played on a piano, or other accompanying instrument. The starting tone or pitch of the first word can also be given.

4. When presenting new songs, groups sometimes need a visual aid to assist with the song texts such as inexpensive song sheets, 35 mm slides, or overhead transparencies. The versatility of each depends on the size of the group and the physical arrangement of the room.

5. A good accompaniment for group singing is a must. Generally a competent pianist should be on hand to maintain the rhythmic flow, the tonality, and the expressiveness of the song. The accompanist often plays a brief introduction which sets the mood and song style.

6. Pace each song session to keep and hold a high interest level in the group. Try not to dwell too long on any single song—especially if it is new. Long or difficult new songs need not be perfected in one session. Present them a little at a time by adding clapping to the rhythm, whistling a portion, or humming along on a verse until it becomes familiar. Eventually, it will be one of the group's "old favorites."

7. When introducing a new round, teach it first as a unison song. Be cautious about dividing it into a round too soon, or using too many sections for round singing. Two or three sections are sufficient. Each section should sing the round as many times as there are sections into which the group has been divided.

8. Many singing groups enjoy song sessions which are built around a theme or topic, such as "Christmas in Many Lands"; "Songs of National Origin"; "A Trip Around the World"; "Tin Pan Alley"; "Names in Songs" ("Bill Bailey," "Lili Marlene," "Alfie," etc.).

9. It often adds to a song session if the leader can intersperse anecdotes about the songs. Good leaders usually collect interesting bits of information for this purpose. But, regardless of how interesting these are, the use of verbal remarks should be kept at a minimum.

10. Interest is high when talented members of the group perform special solos or ensembles. It adds variety to group singing and provides an opportunity to "launch" the male quartet or ladies' sextet.

CONDUCTING PATTERNS

The ability to conduct basic patterns is an important requisite for all song leaders. There are, however, occasions when formal conducting can be set aside in favor of more informal ways of keeping time. Some of these might include simple time beating, foot tapping, finger snapping, body gesture, accompaniment, or lead-in cues, such as "one, two, ready—sing."

Formal conducting patterns relate directly to the meter signature of a song. Below are examples of meter signatures and the manual pattern used in conducting each.[2] A song to practice each conducting pattern is also included.

Meter Signature   *Conducting Pattern*

2   6
4 or fast 8   (duple in 2's)

Under the Spreading Chestnut Tree

ENGLAND

Un - der the spread - ing chest - nut tree,

When I held you on my knee,

We were hap - py as can be,

Un - der the spread - ing chest - nut tree.

Additional songs in duple meter which may be conducted with the above pattern:

Skip to My Lou
Are You Sleeping
Shoo Fly
Yankee Doodle
Kookaburra
This Old Man
Dixie
Sailing, Sailing
When Johnny Comes Marching Home
Silent Night

Old Mac Donald Had a Farm
Jingle Bells
She'll Be Comin' Round the Mountain
Lightly Row
The Marines' Hymn
Oh Susannah
Row, Row, Row Your Boat
Pussy Cat
Over the River and Through the Wood

2. Music and texts of all songs listed are in Dallin-Dallin *Heritage Songster*, published by Wm. C. Brown Company Publishers, Dubuque, Iowa, 1969.

Meter Signature		Conducting Pattern
3	3	
4	2 (triple in 3's)	

Music Alone Shall Live

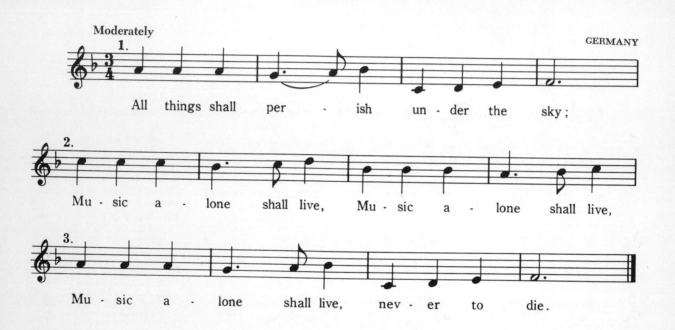

All things shall per - ish un - der the sky;

Mu - sic a - lone shall live, Mu - sic a - lone shall live,

Mu - sic a - lone shall live, nev - er to die.

GERMANY

Himmel und Erde müssen vergehn;
Aber die Musica, aber die Musica,
Aber die Musica, bleiben bestehn.

Additional songs in triple meter which may be conducted with the above pattern:

America
Oh, Where, Oh, Where Has My Little Dog
    Gone?
Prayer of Thanksgiving
Lavender's Blue Dilly, Dilly
Happy Birthday to You
Come Thou Almighty King
Oh, How Lovely Is the Evening
Sidewalks of New York
On Top of Old Smoky

The Star Spangled Banner
Skaters' Waltz (Waldteufel)
Sweet Betsy from Pike
We Wish You a Merry Christmas
The First Noel
Down in the Valley
Clementine
Faith of Our Fathers
Daisy Bell

Meter Signature   *Conducting Pattern*

4
4   (Quadruple in 4's)

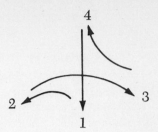

Aura Lee

U.S.

1. As the black-bird in the spring, 'Neath the wil-low tree,_____

Sat and piped, I heard him sing, Sing - ing Au-ra Lee.

Chorus

Au - ra Lee, Au - ra Lee, Maid of gold-en hair,

Sun-shine came a - long with thee, And swal-lows in the air.

2. In her blush the rose was born,
Music when she spoke,
In her eyes the glow of morn
Into splendor broke.

Additional songs in quadruple meter conducted with the above pattern:

America, the Beautiful
All Through the Night
Long, Long Ago
A-Hunting We Will Go
O Come All Ye Faithful
Alouette
Jacob's Ladder
Auld Lang Syne

I've Been Working on the Railroad
Twinkle, Twinkle Little Star
Hark the Herald Angels Sing
Red River Valley
Crusaders' Hymn
Swing Low, Sweet Chariot
London Bridge

There are some songs written in $\frac{6}{8}$ meter which are intended to be sung at a moderate to slow tempo. These songs require the conducting pattern shown below if and when they are sung slowly.

Meter Signature

$\frac{6}{8}$ (Sextuple in 6's)

Conducting Pattern

Greensleeves

ENGLISH

What child is this __ who came to rest __ on Ma-ry's lap __ is sleep - ing And an - gels greet __ with an - thems sweet __ while shep - herds voice __ are sing - ing. __ This, this __ is Christ the King __ Whom An - gels guard __ and shep - herds sing This, this __ is

Greensleeves

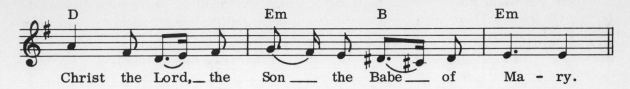

Christ the Lord,__ the Son __ the Babe__ of Ma - ry.

Additional songs in sextuple meter which may be conducted with the above pattern:

We Three Kings   Silent Night
Sweet and Low   Greensleeves

One of the important responsibilities of a song leader is to bring all of the singers together for a clean, secure start on the first word of a song. This is comparatively easy when songs begin on a down-beat (usually the first beat of the measure). The leader may conduct one full measure to establish the tempo and direct the singers to begin on the first beat of his second conducted measure. Sometimes he can say, "One, two, ready, sing" in strict cadence as a verbal starting cue. Or, he may give a clear preparatory beat in strict rhythm on the last beat of the measure preceding entrance.

However, when a song begins on the up-beat (usually the last beat in a measure), entrances are frequently weak and ragged. One way to overcome this is for the leader to conduct all beats occurring prior to the entrance up-beat. Until the group becomes used to this technique, the leader can count as he conducts. The following common examples can be used for practice. These are upbeats on the third and fourth beats of the measure.

Songs starting on an up-beat in a 3 or triple rhythm:

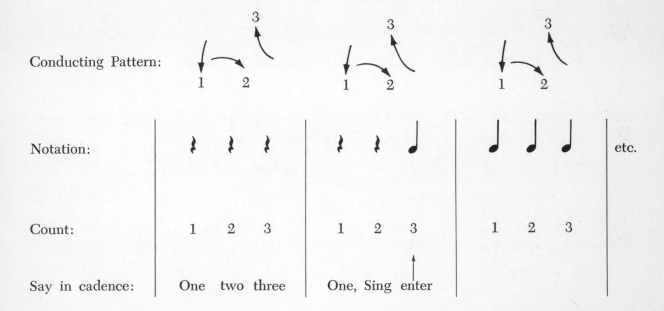

The Holly and the Ivy

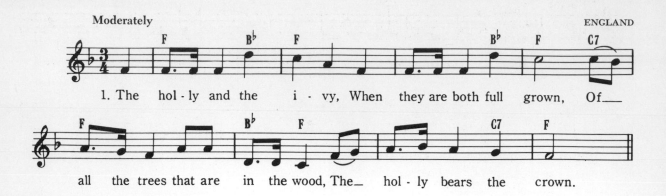

Songs starting on an up-beat in a 4 or quadruple rhythm:

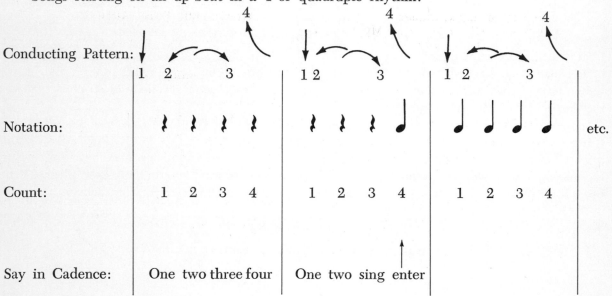

Auld Lang Syne

ROBERT BURNS

SCOTLAND

Auld Lang Syne

For auld lang syne, my dear, For auld lang syne; We'll take a cup of kind - ness yet for auld lang syne.

Additional songs starting on the last (up) beat of the measure:

America, The Beautiful
On Top of Old Smoky
The Star Spangled Banner
Oh Where, Oh Where Has My Little Dog Gone?
Prayer of Thanksgiving
The First Noel
Happy Birthday to You
The Marines' Hymn
Clementine

Bingo
The More We Get Together
Flow Gently Sweet Afton
Sweet Betsy from Pike
We Wish You a Merry Christmas
Greensleeves
Oh, A-Hunting We Will Go
Oh Come All Ye Faithful
Oh Susannah
Red River Valley

ADDING SIMPLE HARMONY PARTS TO SONGS

Harmonic enrichment can turn an otherwise routine song session into a rewarding and sensitive experience. Community singing in any recreational situation seems to take on a special quality when groups sing in harmony. There are numerous ways to add simple patterns to familiar songs thereby producing harmonic effects. Perhaps the easiest harmonic effects. Perhaps the easiest harmonic experience is antiphonal singing. The following is a well-known example of answer-back or "antiphonal" singing.

Old Texas

They've plowed and fenced my cattle range,
And the people there are all so strange.
I'll take my horse, I'll take my rope,
And hit the trail upon a lope.
Say adios to the Alamo,
And turn my head toward Mexico.

For further enrichment, simple repeated patterns (*ostinati*), such as shown below, can be sung or played throughout.

Sing:
Play:
(Woodblock,
bells or bongo)

Clop, clop   Clop, clop etc.

The following *ostinati* patterns may be added to "Home on the Range." Indicate the pattern that fits with the words of the melody by using either a visual cue or hand signal. The number of the pattern is indicated above the appropriate sections of the text.

(1)

Rid-ing   a - long

(2)

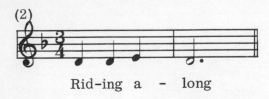

Rid-ing   a - long

(3)

Rid-ing   a - long

(1)   (2)
Oh give me a home where the buffalo roam,
      (1)   (1)
Where the deer and the antelope play;
      (1)   (2)
Where seldom is heard a discouraging word,
      (1)   (3)
And the skies are not cloudy all day.

(1)   (1)
Home, home on the range
      (1)   (1)
Where the dear and the antelope play;
      (1)   (2)
Where seldom is heard a discouraging word,
      (1)   (3)
And the skies are not cloudy all day.

GOSHEN COLLEGE LIBRARY
GOSHEN, INDIANA   46526

Easy tenor and bass parts can also be added. The following is a good example which is suitable for all age groups. Harmony parts may be added one at a time in a rhythmic fashion. Chording instruments are also very appropriate.[3]

Rock-a-my-Soul

3. Arrangements as found in Sally Monsour and Margaret Perry, *A Junior High School Music Handbook,* 2nd ed. (Englewood Cliffs, New Jersey: Prentice-Hall, Inc., 1970), pp. 81-82.

Rock-a-my-Soul

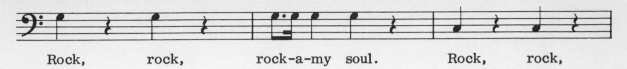

Rock,   rock,   rock-a-my soul.   Rock,   rock,

rock-a-my   soul,   Oh,   rock-a-my   soul.

A parody on a familiar song can add fun and satisfaction to recreational singing. These are especially useful during holiday seasons. If the singing group is made up of youngsters, they will be anxious to make up their own sets of words. The following may serve as examples.

Tune: "Are You Sleeping?"[4]
(Thanksgiving)

Turkey 'n' dressing, Turkey 'n' dressing
Pumpkin pie, Pumpkin pie.
Everybody's humming, Thanksgiving is coming
Yum, yum, yum; yum, yum, yum.

Tune: "Did You Ever See a Lassie?"
(Halloween)

Oh, once I had a pumpkin, a pumpkin, a pumpkin
Oh, once I had a pumpkin, with no face at all.
With no eyes, and no nose and no mouth and no teeth,
Oh, once I had a pumpkin with no face at all.
So I made a Jack-o-lantern, Jack-o-lantern, Jack-o-lantern
So I made a Jack-o-lantern with a big funny face.
With big eyes, and big nose and big mouth and big teeth.
So I made a Jack-o-lantern with a big funny face.

Tune: "Farmer in the Dell"
(Halloween)

The witch rides tonight, the witch rides tonight.
Hi Ho it's Halloween, the witch rides tonight.
The witch takes a bat, the witch takes a bat,
Hi Ho it's Halloween, the witch takes a bat.
The bat takes a cat, the bat takes a cat,
Hi Ho it's Halloween, the bat takes a cat.
The cat scares the ghost, the cat scares the ghost,
Hi Ho it's Halloween, the cat scares the ghost.
The ghosts dance around, the ghosts dance around
Hi Ho it's Halloween, the ghosts dance around, Boo!

4. Sybal Parr, Atlanta Georgia. Used by permission.

The literature for group singing includes every type of song. To assist the recreational song leader, lists of songs by category may be found in Appendix H. The songs which follow are good examples for group singing. Practice them for using various techniques for rote learning and for song conducting and leadership.

Sing Together

Vive L'amour

Vive L'amour

Vi - ve la vi - ve la vi - ve l'a - mour Vi - ve l'a - mour,

Vi - ve l'a - mour, Vi - ve la com - pa - gnie!_____

2. A friend on the left and a friend on the right, Vive la compagnie!
   In willing endeavor our hands we unite, Vive la compagnie!
3. Should time or occasion compel us to part, Vive la compagnie!
   These days shall forever enliven the heart, Vive la compagnie!

We're All Together Again

ENGLAND

We're all to - geth - er a - gain, we're here, we're

here!_____ We're all to - geth - er a - gain, we're

here, we're here!_____ Who knows

when we'll be all to - geth - er a - gain, sing - ing,

"All to - geth - er a - gain, we're here, we're here!"_____

Las Mañanitas

Leisurely

MEXICO

As of old, we bring a song, a greet - ing
gay at ear - ly dawn; Wak - en, friend, and join our
sing - ing, O hear the mu - sic we bring.
I'll step out of doors at dawn - ing, I'll
climb up a mag - ic stair, And bring down the stars of
morn - ing to make a crown for your hair.

Estas son las mañanitas que cantaba el Rey David,
Pero no eran tanbonitas como las cantan aquí.
Despierta, mi bién, despierta, mira que ya amaneció;
Ya los pajarillos cantan, la luna ya se metió.
Despierta, mi bién, despierta, mira que ya amaneció;
Ya los pajarillos cantan, la luma ya se metió.
Estas son las mañanitas que cantaba el Rey David,
Pero no eran tanbonitas como las cantan aquí.

Jacob's Ladder

SPIRITUAL

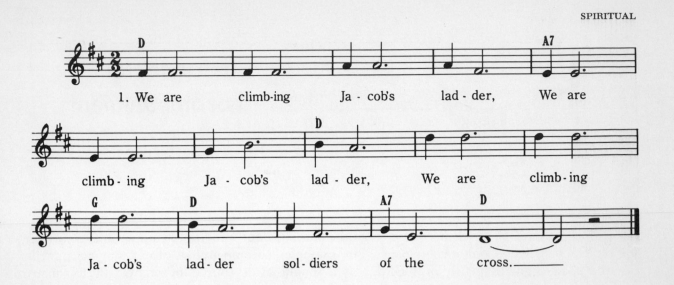

2. Every round goes higher, higher, etc.
3. Brother, do you love my Jesus? etc.
4. If you love Him, you must serve Him, etc.
5. We are climbing higher, higher, etc.

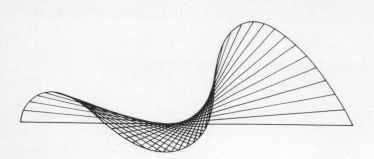

10.

instrumental
accompaniment

The instruments which accompany group music-making provide an important means for musical achievement and involvement.[1] For example, accompanying group singing on the autoharp, uke, guitar, piano, or recorder, is a sought after source of enjoyment for many people. In fact, most recreation programs offer group instrument instruction for beginners of different ages.[2]

THE AUTOHARP

Probably the simplest accompanying instrument to play is the autoharp. It is easily mastered and can be self-taught. Because of its size and weight, it is an ideal instrument for recreational use. Its portability provides a means of accompaniment on hikes, around the campfire, in the recreational hall, at the beach, or around the dinner table.

Besides being portable, it is relatively inexpensive when compared to a piano, violin, or accordion. The upkeep is no problem, and the tuning of the instrument is simple.

The autoharp is equipped with all the accessories for playing and tuning. Several picks are included to produce various degrees and kinds of sound effects. A shoulder strap is also supplied for playing while walking or standing.

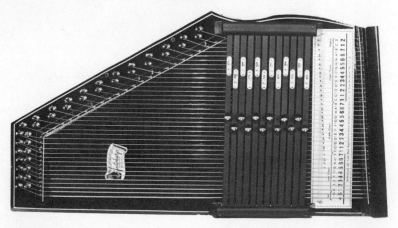

Autoharp is the registered Trade Mark of Oscar Schmidt International, Inc., Jersey City, New Jersey.

1. Special mention should be made of a comprehensive book on using instruments of all types in musical situations: Marguerite V. Hood, *Teaching Rhythm and Using Classroom Instruments* (Englewood Cliffs, New Jersey: Prentice-Hall, Inc., 1970).
2. For a listing of sources on playing instruments, see Appendix D, p. 117.

Playing the Autoharp. The autoharp is usually played on the lap or on a table in front of the player. The wide part of the instrument is at the player's right. The left hand is used to depress the bars before the chord is strummed. The bars are clearly labeled identifying the various chords the instrument is capable of producing. (A twelve bar instrument is usually sufficient for recreational purposes.) The player's right hand strums away from the body, across the wire strings on either side of the bar rack. The sound created by strumming on the left side of the bar rack has a deep, full quality. The number of times the player strums depends on the beat pattern of the song and the player's own sense of rhythm, but the chord button must be changed when the harmony changes are indicated in the music.

Tuning the Autoharp. A tuning wrench is provided with each instrument. This wrench can easily be applied to the clearly marked pegs in order to tighten or loosen the attached string until the sound (pitch) corresponds to the pitch on a piano or tuning pipe.

Finding Chords on An Autoharp. On the twelve-bar autoharp the player can create accompaniments for three major keys (C, G, and F) and two minor keys (d, and a). Each of these keys has three bars which, when depressed, will create a tonic, subdominant and dominant-seventh chord (I, IV, V₇). The player must firmly press the bar representing the chord and then, with his right hand, strum the wire strings away from the body. (Most editions of recreation songs have the chord symbols printed over the word or beat of the measure where a chord change is required.)

The following song is an illustration. Sing along and strum as each chord change is indicated. The slanted lines next to the chord symbols indicate the strumming rhythm. Continue strumming in rhythm on each slanted line, look ahead, change chords when indicated, and continue strumming.

Down in the Valley

AMERICAN FOLK SONG

THE UKULELE AND FOLK GUITAR

Both the ukulele and guitar are ideal instruments for recreational use. In fact, they are probably the most popular instruments for this purpose. They are both fretted instruments, and reinforce the vocal line harmonically without distracting from the audible quality of the vocal tone. The rhythmic effect of strumming helps to maintain the cohesion of the singing group. One player is adequate for small groups, but there may be several players accompanying larger groups.

The ukulele is the easiest of the two instruments to tune and play. It has only four strings while the guitar has six. The uke is tuned by tightening or loosening the pegs until the pitch corresponds with the pitches G, C, E, A on the piano or tuning pipe. (See diagram on page 57.) The "G" string is the one closest to the chin when holding the instrument in a traditional position. Some teachers use a simple song-pattern, such as "My dog has fleas" on the tuning pitches as a preliminary experience. It tends to reinforce the pitches of the strings "by ear."

The finger patterns for playing the ukulele are shown on page 57. The beginning problems will result from changing finger positions rapidly enough to maintain the rhythmic flow of the music. It is usual to begin with simple two-chord melodies before advancing to three chords or more.

The guitar is a versatile instrument capable of producing rich sounds. It has six strings tuned to the pitches E, A, D, G, B, and E. (See diagram on page 58.) Strumming patterns and chord symbols accompany many contemporary recreational song collections.

The following song indicates an alternating change between the I and V⁷ chords. The symbols are given in the key of C. An even three-beat strum is appropriate for this song. The beat should be kept steady and the chords should move smoothly from one to the other.

"The More We Get Together"

Traditional

Uke:

C:

G⁷:

Strum on each beat
of the measure:

```
                    C                C         G⁷         C
    3/4  The │ more  we get to │ gether, to │ gether, to │ gether,
                    C                C         G⁷              C
         The │ more  we get to │ gether the │ happier we'll │ be.
                    G⁷               C         G⁷               C
         For │ your  friends are │ my friends, and │ my friends are │ your friends.
                    C                C         G⁷              C
         The │ more  we get to │ gether the │ happier we'll │ be.
```

The following song contains the two chords of C and G⁷ for the guitar. The symbols are given in the key of C. Strum on the first beat of each measure where the chord symbols are indicated. The beats should be kept steady and the chords should move smoothly from one to the other.

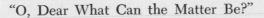

"O, Dear What Can the Matter Be?"

Traditional

Guitar:

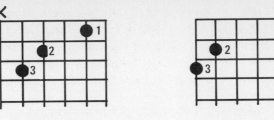

Strum on 1st beat
of the measure:

3/4
C | C | C | C
O, | dear, | what can the | matter be?
G⁷ | G⁷ | G⁷ | G₇
Dear, | dear, | what can the | matter be?
C | C | C | C
O, | dear, | what can the | matter be?
G⁷ | G⁷ | C
Johnny's so | long at the | fair. ‖

Additional songs to practice uke and guitar chords in the key of C.

Joy to the World

ISAAC WATTS

LOWELL MASON

1. Joy to the world! the Lord is come; Let
earth re - ceive her King; Let
ev - 'ry heart pre - pare Him room, And
heav'n and na - ture sing, And heav'n and na - ture sing, And
heav'n and heav'n and na - ture sing.

My Hat

(MEIN HUT)

Moderately   GERMANY

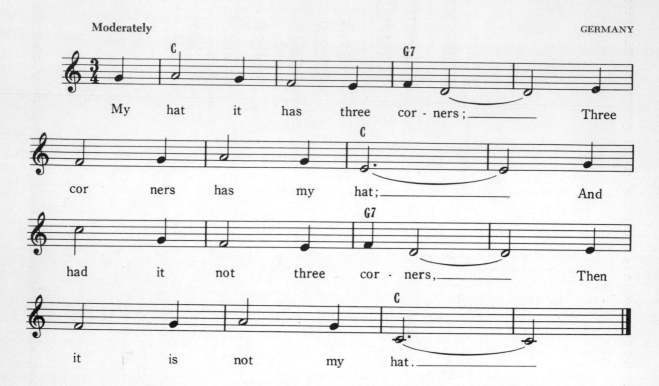

Mein Hut er nicht hat drei Ecken;
Drei Ecken hat mein Hut;

Und hat er nicht drei Ecken;
Denn das ist nicht mein Hut.

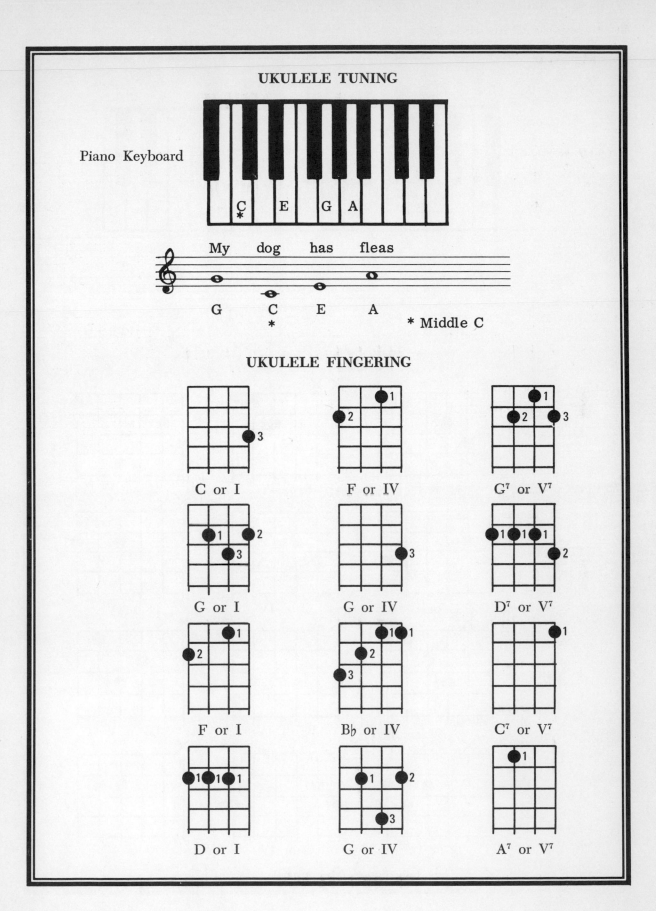

UKULELE TUNING

Piano Keyboard

C *   E   G   A

My   dog   has   fleas

G   C*   E   A   * Middle C

UKULELE FINGERING

C or I   F or IV   G⁷ or V⁷

G or I   G or IV   D⁷ or V⁷

F or I   B♭ or IV   C⁷ or V⁷

D or I   G or IV   A⁷ or V⁷

GUITAR TUNING

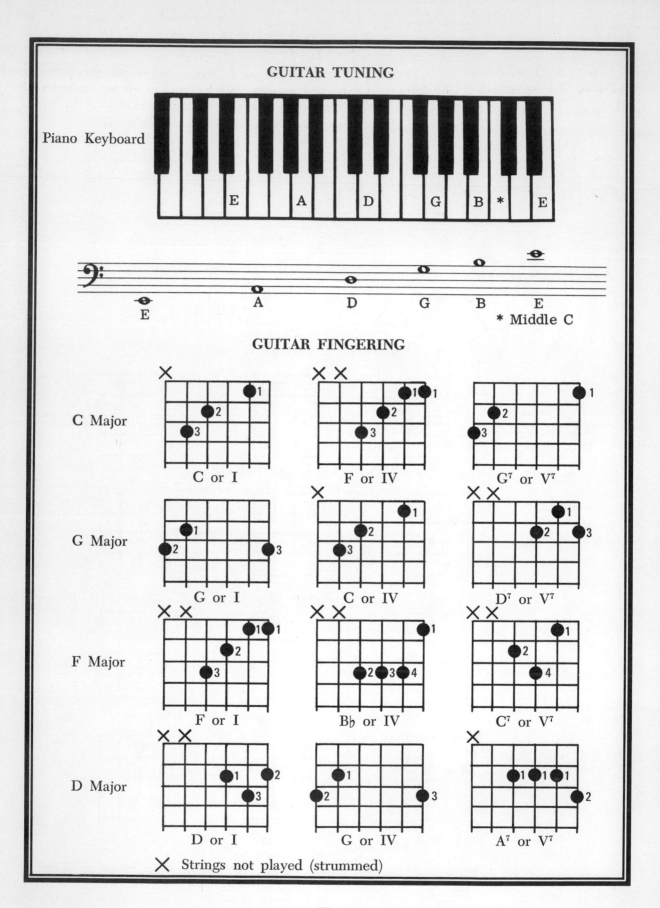

PIANO CHORDING

Simple piano chording can be a great asset to music leaders in a recreational program. Besides playing melody and harmony in a traditional way, the leader can often conduct with the right hand as he plays chords rhythmically with the left. For these purposes, the finger positions of three basic chords (I, IV, and V⁷) in a few keys can be easily mastered.

Each chord consists of three pitches sounded simultaneously. Each chord relates harmonically to the melodic line. The "formula" for moving from a I chord, (tonic) to a V⁷ chord (dominant-seventh) in every major key is the same. The numbers in the formula below represent the degrees of the scale.

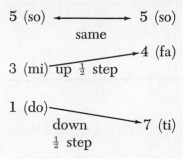

The formula for moving from the I chord (tonic) to the IV chord (sub-dominant) is:

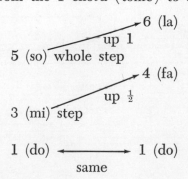

The formula for moving from the IV chord (sub-dominant) to the V⁷ chord (dominant-seventh) is:

In staff notation, the chords in the progression, I-IV-V^7-I, are given below in both treble and bass clefs. These should become automatic as you sing and play the following.

Piano Chords
(Key of C)

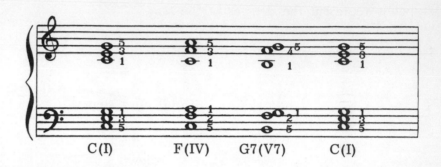

C(I)   F(IV)   G7(V7)   C(I)

Jack and Jill

MOTHER GOOSE RHYME   J. W. ELLIOTT

1. Jack and Jill went up the hill to fetch a pail of wa - ter; Jack fell down and broke his crown, And Jill came tum - bling af - ter.

2. Up Jack got, and home he ran as fast as he could caper,
   There his mother bound his head with vinegar and brown paper.

Piano Chords
(Key of F)

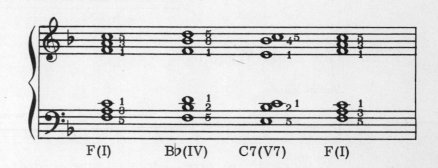

F(I)   B♭(IV)   C7(V7)   F(I)

He's Got the Whole World in His Hands

SPIRITUAL

1. He's got the whole world— in His hands,— He's got the whole world— in His hands,— He's got the whole world— in His hands,— He's got the whole world in His hands.

2. He's got the wind and rain in His hands.
3. He's got that little baby in His hands.
4. He's got you and me in His hands.
5. He's got everybody in His hands.
6. He's got the whole world in His hands.

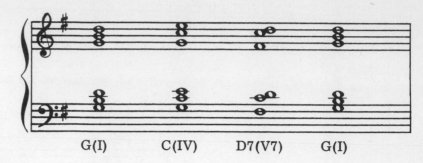

Piano Chords
(Key of G)

G(I)   C(IV)   D7(V7)   G(I)

The Old Brass Wagon

Square dance

MIDWESTERN U. S.

1. Cir-cle to the left, the old brass wag-on, Cir-cle to the left, the old brass wag-on, Cir-cle to the left, the old brass wag-on, You're the one my dar-ling.

2. Circle to the right, the old brass wagon, etc.
3. Swing, oh swing, the old brass wagon, etc.
4. Promenade around, the old brass wagon, etc.
5. Swing your partner, the old brass wagon, etc.
6. Break and swing, the old brass wagon, etc.
7. Promenade in, the old brass wagon, etc.

TEXTS OF MORE FAMILIAR SONGS TO SING AND PLAY

The following songs can be accompanied in any major key which is in a comfortable range for the singers.

DOWN IN THE VALLEY

Kentucky Folk Song

F Major   I   V[7]
Meter   Down in the valley, the valley so low,
9   V[7]   I
8   Hang your head over, hear the winds blow.
                   I   V[7]
          Hear the winds blow, dear, hear the winds blow,
                   V[7]   I
          Hang your head over, hear the winds blow.

CLEMETINE

F Major	I	I	I	V⁷
Meter	In a cavern, in a canyon, excavating for a mine,			
3	V⁷	I	V⁷	I
4	Dwelt a miner, forty-niner, and his daughter Clementine.			
	I	I	I	V⁷
	Oh my darling, Oh my darling, Oh my darling Clementine.			
	V⁷	I	V⁷	I
	You are lost and gone forever, dreadful sorry, Clementine.			

LOOBY LOO

C Major	I	I	I	V⁷
Meter	Here we go looby loo, Here we go looby light,			
2	I	I V⁷		I
4	Here we go looby loo, all on a Saturday night.			

LONDON BRIDGE

C Major	I	I	V⁷	I
Meter	London bridge is falling down, falling down, falling down,			
2	I	I	V⁷ I	
4	London bridge is falling down, my fair lady.			

KUM BA YAH

C Major	I		IV	I
Meter	Kum ba yah, my Lord, Kum ba yah,			
3	I		I	V⁷
4	Kum ba yah, my Lord, Kum ba yah,			
	I		IV	I
	Kum ba yah, my Lord, Kum ba yah,			
	V⁷ I	V⁷	I	
	O Lord—————Kum ba yah.			

ROCKA MY SOUL

Spiritual

C Major	I
Meter	Rocka my soul, in the bosom of Abraham
4	V⁷
4	Rocka my soul, in the bosom of Abraham
	I
	Rocka my soul, in the bosom of Abraham
	V⁷ I
	(clap) Oh, rocka my soul.

THE MORE WE GET TOGETHER

F Major   I   V^7 I

Meter   The more we get together, together, together,

3   I   I   V^7 I

4   The more we get together, the happier we'll be.

          V^7 I   V^7 I

For your friends are my friends and my friends are your friends.

          I   I   V^7 I

The more we get together, the happier we'll be.

SILENT NIGHT

C Major   I   I

Meter   Silent night! Holy night!

6   V^7 I

8   All is calm, all is bright

          IV   I

Round yon virgin mother and child!

          IV   I

Holy infant, so tender and mild,

          V^7 I

Sleep in heavenly peace,

          I   V^7 I

Sleep in heavenly peace,

DIXIE

C Major   I

Meter   Wish I was in the land of cotton,

2   IV

4   Old times there are not forgotten,

          I   V^7 I

Look away, look away, look away Dixie Land.

YANKEE DOODLE

F Major   I   V^7 I   V^7

Meter   Father and I went down to camp along with Captain Goodin,

2   I   IV   V^7 I

4   And there we saw the men and boys as thick as hasty puddin';

        IV   I

Yankee doodle, keep it up, Yankee doodle dandy,

        IV   I   V^7 I

Mind the music and the step and with the girls be handy.

MICHAEL ROW THE BOAT ASHORE

C Major		I	I	IV I
Meter	1. Michael row the boat ashore, Allelujah			
4		I	V⁷	V⁷ I
4	Michael row the boat ashore, Allelujah			

C Major   I   I   IV I

Meter   1. Michael row the boat ashore, Allelujah

4   I V^7 V^7 I

4   Michael row the boat ashore, Allelujah

2. The river is wide and the water is deep, Allelujah (repeat).

3. Sister, help to trim the sail, Allelujah (repeat).

CHORDING WITH RESONATOR BELLS

The use of resonator bells of the individual type can provide a simple and satisfying chording experience. Chording accompaniments to simple songs can be well-played and musically sensitive with the practice of stroking techniques and steady rhythmic playing. In the songs which follow individual persons should each play the bell represented by the appropriate letter name indicated above the melody. It is usually well to sing along and listen carefully as the chords change.

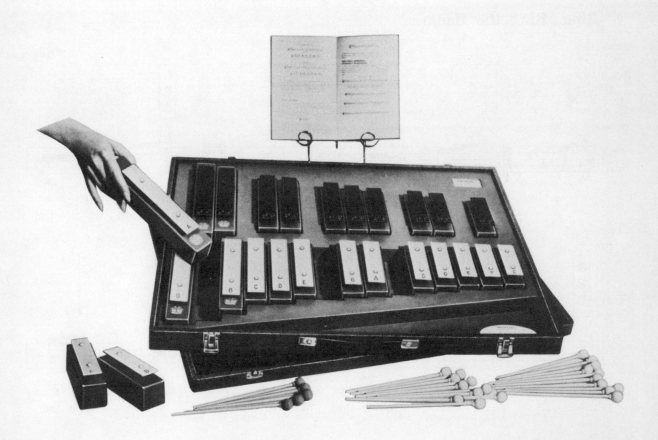

Sandy Land

Resonator Bells

1. Make my liv-ing in sand-y land, Make my liv-ing in sand-y land,

Make my liv-ing in sand-y land, La-dies, fare you well.

Ring, Ring the Banjo

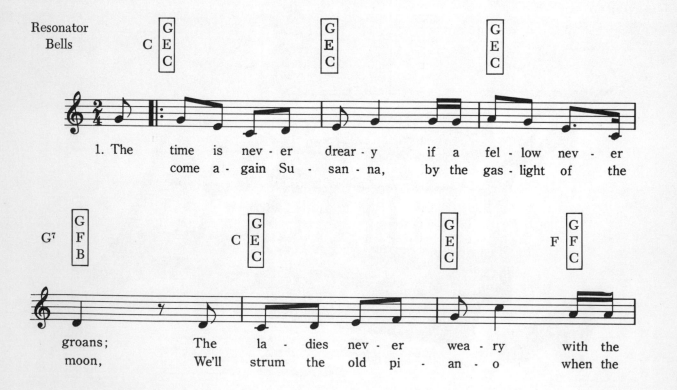

Resonator Bells

1. The time is nev-er drear-y if a fel-low nev-er
come a-gain Su-san-na, by the gas-light of the

groans; The la-dies nev-er wea-ry with the
moon, We'll strum the old pi-an-o when the

Ring, Ring the Banjo

rat - tle   of   the   bones.   Then

ban - jo's   out   of   tune.

Chorus

Ring,   ring   the   ban - jo!   I   like   that   good old   song;

Come a - gain my   true   love,   O   where've you   been   so   long?

2. Oh, never count the bubbles when there's water in the spring,
There's no one who has trouble when he has this song to sing,
The beauties of creation will never lose their charm
While I roam the old plantation with my true love on my arm.

3. My love, I'll have to leave you while the river's running high,
But I will not deceive you, so don't you wipe your eye,
I'm going to make some money, but I'll come another day,
I'll come again, my honey, if I have to work my way.

Drunken Sailor

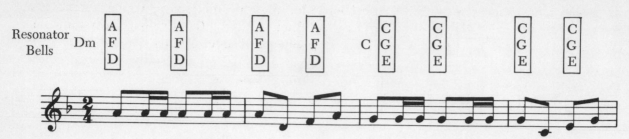

1. What shall we do with a drunk-en sail-or, What shall we do with a drunk-en sail-or,

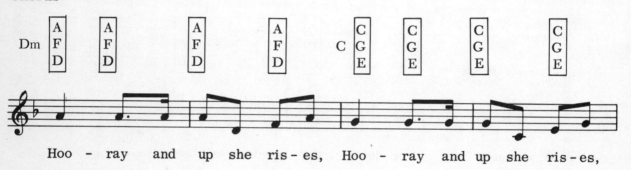

What shall we do with a drunk-en sail - or, Ear-ly in the morn - ing?

Chorus

Hoo - ray and up she ris - es, Hoo - ray and up she ris - es,

Hoo - ray and up she ris - es, Ear - ly in the morn - ing.

2. Put him in the longboat until he's sober, (etc.)
3. Pull out the plug and wet him all over, (etc.)
4. Heave him by the leg in a running bowline.* (etc.)
5. Put him in the scuppers** with a hose-pipe on him, (etc.)
6. Toss him in the brig until he's sober, (etc.)

*Rope to keep sail taut.
**Opening in ship's side for water run off.

SIMPLE "ROCK" PROGRESSIONS

Besides learning simple traditional chords for diatonic folk songs, young people today are very familiar with the musical patterns in "Rock" music. The following rhythmic, harmonic and melodic progressions will add an element of interest to a jam session.

Tambourines repeat this measure throughout:

Drums repeat this measure throughout:

Rhythmic pattern for other instruments or clapping:

Chord patterns for guitar or autoharp:

(each block represents one measure of piano patterns)

C⁷	C⁷	C⁷	C⁷	F⁷	F⁷	F⁷	F⁷	C⁷	C⁷	C⁷	C⁷

G⁷	G⁷	G⁷	G⁷	C⁷	C⁷	C⁷	C⁷

Melodic Patterns for Piano:

As arranged by a graduate class in music education at the University of Michigan, Ann Arbor, Michigan.

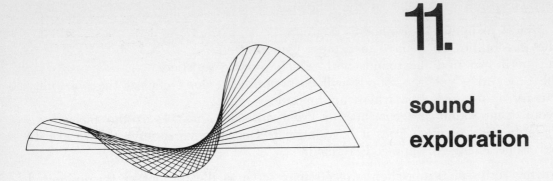

11.

sound exploration

Exploring and organizing sounds into expressive musical entities is suitable for recreational activities, especially with young people. It is a constant and available means for self- and group-initiated experiences. These are highly motivating because they require originality and creation.[1]

The most accessible sounds are those we can produce ourselves, such as singing, humming, and whistling. These are called "self-sounds." With a little thought and experimentation, numerous self-sounds are possible: moaning, hissing, purring, cackling, gasping, murmuring, sighing, sniffing, clicking, etc. The effect of each of these can be altered by variation of pitch, dynamics, and tempo. Other ways of producing self-sounds with parts of the body are by clapping, stamping, clicking fingers, and slapping knees.

In addition, the sounds in the environment, whether indoors or out, provide unending sources for a variety of sounds in creative activities—classroom sounds; sounds in the home; sounds of objects or machinery; sounds of nature; various speeds of tape recorded sounds. All of these are open-ended sources for composition and creativity.

Standard musical instruments provide additional media for creative purposes. These instruments, including the piano, may be played in many ways through experimentation so that sounds can be summoned other than those generally associated with the instrument. Original instruments made by students themselves are also effective and should be incorporated into compositional experiences.

For many recreational purposes, such as playgrounds and community centers, group compositional projects are sources of satisfaction. Teams may work simultaneously on a given sound problem. Leaders and group organization should remain flexible. It is often best to begin with a simple project before proceeding to more extended pieces. An example of a simple team project might be: create a fifteen-second piece which uses only two instruments of different registers (high, low). Select one instrument to maintain a repeated rhythmic pattern (*ostinato*) throughout.

Sources for inspiration in creative composition may also include dramatic ideas such as events, poems, or commercials. Mood music can be created to enrich a story, or as "atmosphere" for various holidays.

1. Several of the creative ideas in this section are taken from *Music Bulletin # 1: Classroom Composition: An Approach to Music Learnings* by Eugene W. Troth (Cincinnati, Ohio: American Book Company, 1970). Used by permission.

Before the groups divide for their compositional work, they may need suggestions on a procedure for their group work, such as the following:

1. Read the project assignment together as a group.
2. Discuss the possibilities for sounds to express your project.
3. Experiment until you find the sounds with which you are satisfied.
4. Decide the order in which the sounds will be organized. (Don't neglect the possibility for spontaneity or improvisation where appropriate.)
5. Perform your composition and continue to listen critically. Ask: Does the piece have a good beginning and ending? Does it have interest? Does it have variety? Do we like it? How could it be changed, improved, refined?

The following series of composition projects may serve as illustrations of the unlimited possibilities within this area. These should be limited to 1-3 minutes each.

Project 1:
Goal: Creat a musical abstraction of a haunted house.
Sounds: 1 vocal sound, 2 instrumental sounds, 1 spoken word, 1 body sound
Limitations: Contrasts should be obvious. Use slow-fast-slow pattern for tempo.

Project 2:
Goal: Create a musical mood piece for the words: "Let the Sunshine In."
Sounds: 1 autoharp, 3 other classroom instruments, 1 vocal sound
Limitations: Start slowly and softly and gradually increase both dynamics and tempo.

Project 3:
Goal: Create a musical "picture" of the following text:

Praise ye the god of gold;
Praise ye the god of silver;
Praise ye the god of wood;
Praise ye the god of stone;
Praise ye the god of brass;
Praise ye the gods;

Sounds: 4 instruments, 1 vocal sound
Limitations: Use the dynamics level of loud-soft-loud as an overall pattern; start with one instrument.

Project 4:
Goal: Create a musical "Picture" of the poem below.
Sounds: 1 body sound, 1 vocal sound, 3 instruments
Limitations: Begin with one sound, adding others one at a time

Slowly slowly the drip drip drip
Splick splick . . . splock of coming rain
And then the roar
As icily cold needles penetrate the skin of things
To the very very bone core.[2]

. . . Jennifer Lloyd

2. From *The Wind and the Rain.* Collected by Richard Lewish with photographs by Helen Buttfield. New York: Simon and Schuster, Inc., 1968, p. 18.

Project 5:

Goal: Create a musical description of the "feeling" sense (tactile) of the objects given you. (Suggestions: cotton, pine cone, aluminum foil.)

Sounds: 3 classroom instruments, 2 vocal sounds

Limitations: Begin and end with the softest sound you use in your composition.

Project 6:

Goal: Create a musical fabric using the following words as inspiration: "snap, crackle, pop"

Sounds: 2 homemade sounds, 1 instrumental sound.

Limitations: The sounds must always be presented in the word order above; sounds may overlap and variety may be gained by tempo and dynamics.

Project 7:

Goal: Create a sound description of the mood of "Christmas is here."

Sounds: Bells, 2 body sounds, 1 classroom instrument.

Limitations: The piece must have three sections alternating somehow from loud-soft-loud.

Project 8:

Goal: Create a sound study based on the life of an astronaut."

Sounds: 2 classroom instruments, 2 body sounds, 1 vocal sound.

Limitations: Start with many sounds together and gradually diminish into silence.

Project 9:

Goal: Create a sound description of a nature walk entitled: "Alone with God."

Sounds: Self-sounds only.

Limitations: "Silences" within the composition will be obvious.

SCIENCE AND SOUND

Many experiences relate sound with scientific principles. The following lesson outline demonstrates the concept of wind-instrument sound production.

Materials:
1. Eight *no-return* pop bottles
2. Funnel
3. Bucket of water
4. Cup
5. Mallet
6. Food coloring

Objectives:
1. Recognition and creation of a diatonic scale.
2. Pitch discrimination.
3. Understanding of the scientific aspects of pitch.
4. Ability to apply a scale in the student's own composition.
5. Recognition of melodic direction.

Procedures:
1. Place the empty bottles on a table at random. Ask the class, "How can we make an instrument from these bottles?" Some possible answers are: Fill the bottles to different levels and either strike the bottles or blow into them.

2. Take a couple of bottles and fill some of them with varying levels of water. First strike the bottles then blow into them. The pitch will be opposite, in other words, the empty bottle will be the highest pitch when struck and the lowest pitch when blown into. Ask the students why this is so. If they do not know then ask them what is vibrating to make the sound. Then discuss length of the vibrating source in relation to the pitch. (This could launch into a discussion of other instruments and their sound sources.)

3. Many instruments have enough selections of pitch to create a scale. How could we create a scale on these bottles? Of course by putting different levels of water in them. Use the blower end of a vacuum cleaner as a constant source of air. Have a student regulate the vacuum, another student filling the bottles and the class determining whether the tones are sharp or flat and how to correct them.

Possible Uses and Lessons for this Creation:

1. Listen to songs with a diatonic scale in them: "Joy to the World," "Do-Re-Mi" from the *Sounds of Music* etc.
2. Students can create an *ostinato* on the bottles to a song they know.
3. Students can create their own composition with the bottles. (It would also be very easy for them to practice at home.)
4. Students can make two or more sets of bottle scales for harmony. (This could be related to a pipe organ.)
5. From this creation it would be easy to transfer the sounds to the staff.
6. From this, a unit on instrumental sound source and the basic principles of vibration and pitch could be presented.

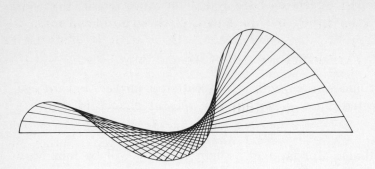

12.

choral
speaking

Choral speaking includes a wide variety of interesting and expressive activities for recreational use. By definition, it is the organization of spoken words into meaningful patterns. Choral speaking is similar to singing except that a speaking voice is substituted for a singing tone. Exciting and artistic effects may thus be achieved. This is especially true when spoken words and word-groupings are combined with musical or self-sounds.[1]

Choral speaking groups are especially suitable to recreational settings because they allow for involvement by persons of any age. These may be in single age groups or in combined groups of different ages. The high, light registers of children's voices are often combined with the qualities and ranges of adult voices.

The size of choral speaking groups depends on the practicalities of the recreational situation. All who are interested should somehow be accommodated. In this sense, the basic goal of recreation, which is pleasure and enjoyment, will have been taken into consideration. However, when selection is made for other reasons, it is usual to have twelve or more persons in a group. Less than twelve limits the possibilities for fullness and variety.

Effective choral speaking depends upon the appropriate classification of the voices themselves.[2] Each member of the group should be heard individually and placed in either the light, medium, or dark category. For this purpose, the leader directs each person to speak a phrase, such as: "Hello, everybody. One two, three, four, five" in a normal, natural speaking voice. All members of the group should be called upon to assist in voice description and classification. This procedure initiates the importance of attentive listening which is prerequisite to good choral speaking. It also tends to create a "game" spirit and the feeling of group dependency.

As soon as individuals are classified, they should be seated in groups. The physical arrangement or placement is not important except in the context of the composition being performed. Once in classified groups, each group should recite the "testing" phrase in turn. Interest is immediately sparked as all witness the results of spoken group "color."

Choral speaking material for both informal occasions and public performance is only limited by the imagination of those involved. Compositions may range from a brief rendition of the local news to an epic poem. In the beginning, however, it is best to begin with simple word patterns and sound combinations which can be enriched by the use of dynamic levels, accents, and rhythmic manipulation.

1. See p. 71 for a description and listing of self-sounds.
2. The ability to "carry a tune" does not necessarily affect voice classification in a speaking group.

The following is an illustration of a choral speaking presentation using a newspaper weather report. Instruments and/or sound effects may be added for variety and expressive power.

WEATHER REPORT   By J. B. and S. M.

Weather Report: Monday will be fair and warmer with a few scattered showers toward evening. Lowered temperatures expected Tuesday with a ten percent chance of snow.

Choral Speaking

Enter all voices (very low in strict rhythm): Monday will be fair, Monday will be fair, Monday will be fair.

Enter solo light voice (little child quality): Monday will be warmer and warmer and warmer.

Enter medium voices (raucausly in loud voice): scattered showers toward evening (pause).

Enter all voices (moderately): Monday will be. . .

Enter light voices (loud): fair and warm. . .

Enter heavy voices (louder): with scattered showers toward evening (pause).

Enter medium and light voices sustaining the vowel sound "Ooooo" throughout the following entrance.

Enter heavy voices (dirge-like): lowered temperatures expected Tuesday, lowered temperatures expected Tuesday.

Enter light voices (fast and shrill): with a ten percent chance of snow.

Enter all voices (loud, gradually diminishing): ohhhhh.

More extended compositions can be created using the names of cities or counties. These may take on fun and interest when local states are used. The following is an example from South Carolina.

SOUTH CAROLINA!   By J. B. and S. M.

Enter light voices (fast and soft): Lancaster, Beaufort and Pawleys Island

Enter medium voices (same tempo a little louder): Orangeburg, Camden and Aiken

Enter light voices (very slowly): Greenwood, Spartanburg, Walterboro

Enter heavy voices (whispered): St. Matthews, St. George, Bishopville

Enter light voices, medium and loud voices (in rapid succession, very loud): Columbia!!

Enter solo medium voice: Bamberg

Enter solo heavy voice: Bennettsville (in rapid succession)

Enter solo light voice: Batesburg

Enter light voices (chant softly and gradually increase in volume):

CHARLESTON (During this chant, the medium voices speak deliberately): Myrtle Beach, Marion, Mullins, McCormick

Enter solo light voice (piercingly): Killian!!

Enter heavy voices chanting: Columbia as medium voices and light voices chant: Charleston. Both groups gradually increase speed and volume until a frenetic effect is reached ending abruptly with a very loud cymbal crash.

Short poems, sometimes created by the groups themselves, are effective for fast-pace renditions in choral speaking. The following is an example.

LAMENT
By J. B.

Heavy voices: I hate to say goodbye to you;
Medium voices: It's such a stupid thing to do.
Light voices: For we have barely said hello;
All voices: And now you have to up and go!

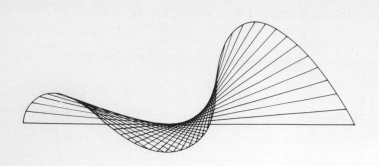

13.

dramatic movement and traditional dancing

Dramatic movement is one type of rhythmic response that lends itself very well to recreational activities. It provides a means for improvisation, mime, storytelling, musical response, and accompaniment. Ideas for dramatized movement range from everyday experiences, such as a simple gesture or greeting, to a dramatized composition based on a poem or painting.[1] The subject chosen will naturally depend upon the age and interest of the participants.

Probably the most common starting point for dramatic movement is pantomime. Simple gestures or ideas are translated into motion and then extended to express a total concept—no matter how small or short. Common gestures, or actions which may be translated into pantomime are: shaking hands, waving, winking, eating, sleeping, crying, laughing, praying, applauding. These may be expanded by transferring the movement to another part of the body, changing the rhythm of the gesture, increasing or diminishing the size of the movement, or adding other body parts to the movement. Step patterns may also be added to expand the total action as follows:

Shake Hands:

1. Turn to someone near you and shake right hands, left hands.
2. Take this person as your partner; everyone form a circle.
3. Face your partner and shake right hands again. Walk around the circle shaking hands alternately right and left with each person you meet. (Half of the children will move clockwise and half counter-clockwise as in a grand right and left.)
4. Do the same thing, substituting a polka for a walk.
5. Do it again. Extend your hand, but don't touch anyone.

The senses of touch, taste, and smell are wonderful sources for dramatic movement. The following group activity involves the sense of touch.

WHAT DO YOU FEEL

Thoughts to Teach By

Choose objects having different shapes and textures.

Encourage children to devise their own movements, without imitating their classmates.

---

1. Several illustrated lessons for dramatized movement may be found in *Rhythm in Music and Dance for Children* by Sally Monsour, Marilyn Cohen and Patricia Lindell © 1966 by Wadsworth Publishing Company, Belmont, California 94002. "What do you Feel?" and "The Machine" are taken directly from this book reprinted with permission of the publisher.

PROCEDURE	HINTS
1. Place items with different shapes and textures into separate paper bags.	Rough, hard, smooth, soft—corn cob, sandpaper, ice cube, velvet, fur, feathers.
2. Divide into groups. Give each group a bag containing a different item.	Direct them not to look inside.
3. Each person in the group reaches into the bag, one at a time to feel the contents.	The stimulus for movement should be entirely tactile.
4. Each person devises his own movement based on the texture of the object as he felt it.	If you do not wish to devote much time to the lesson, this part may be improvised, with steps 4 and 5 combined.
5. All in the same group perform together.	They should not attempt to produce organized group movement. However, individual movements will probably be of a similar quality.
6. After the group performs, show the objects from which the movement has evolved.	This will clarify the exercise and satisfy the children's curiosity.

Games, sports, nature, animals, mass media, and the events surrounding mechanization and urban living are all excellent sources for groups to use in creating dramatized compositions, dances, and plays. Sounds are usually combined with extended dramatic ideas so that the composite can be very rewarding and often artistic. Involvement is at a high level if groups are allowed to initiate their own ideas. Giving little hints of ways to begin, material assistance, or help when things get "bogged" down, will naturally be the role of the leader or teacher. But, as far as possible, participants should explore most experiences on their own.

The project which follows illustrates a combined activity on mechanized movement entitled: "The Machine."[2] It includes dramatic idea, movement exploration, and sounds. It could also enrich concepts of rhythm reading.

THE MACHINE

Write the chart below on the blackboard and refer to it throughout the lesson. If the group is unfamiliar with notation, omit that part of the chart and allow them to formulate their own rhythmic patterns, disregarding notation. Provide the conventional instruments listed on the chart, or simulated ones such as kitchen utensils, for group exploration and mechanical sounds and background in sound exploration.

Suggest that the group examine machines (ditto, typewriter, etc.) and improvise their own sounds, patterns, and movements.

		RHYTHMIC PATTERNS	
SOUND	SUGGESTED MOVEMENT	YOUNGER GROUP	OLDER GROUP
Sand blocks	Horizontal lever—arm	$\frac{2}{4}$ ♩ ♩ | ♩ 𝄽	$\frac{5}{4}$ 𝅗𝅥 ♩ ♩ ♩ ||

2. Listen to selections such as "Steel Foundry," Mossolov Recording: Sounds of New Music, Folkways (FX 6160).

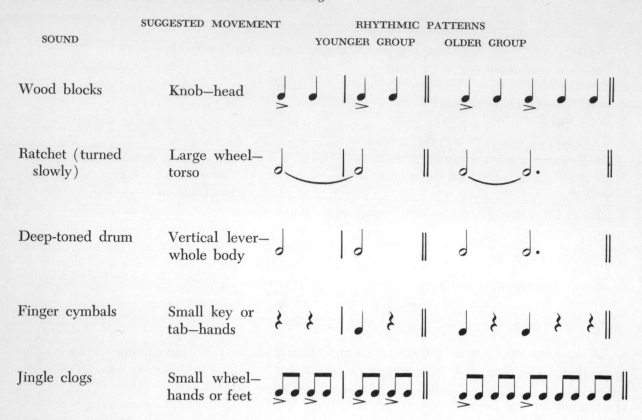

SOUND	SUGGESTED MOVEMENT	RHYTHMIC PATTERNS YOUNGER GROUP	OLDER GROUP
Wood blocks	Knob—head		
Ratchet (turned slowly)	Large wheel—torso		
Deep-toned drum	Vertical lever—whole body		
Finger cymbals	Small key or tab—hands		
Jingle clogs	Small wheel—hands or feet		

TRADITIONAL DANCE STEPS

There are many occasions in a recreation program when the basic patterns of traditional dance steps are needed. Although these are usually included in dance descriptions, they are not generally given in concise form in one place. It is with this in mind that the authors are including them here. The rhythm and dance references at the end of this section will often refer to several of these traditional steps[3] either as a part of the dance or as the basis for the entire dance.

Buzz Step (turning in place)

word cue		step	push	step	push
step pattern		R	L	R	L
rhythmic pattern	2/4	♩.	♪	♩.	♪
underlying beat		—	—	—	—

3. Taken from *Rhythm in Music and Dance for Children*, Ibid., p. 79-80.

Jig

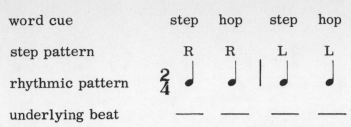

word cue		step	hop	step	hop
step pattern		R	R	L	L
rhythmic pattern	2/4	♩	♩	♩	♩
underlying beat		—	—	—	—

Mazurka

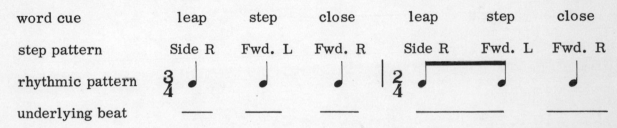

word cue		step	close	hop	step	close	hop
step pattern		R	L	L	R	L	L
rhythmic pattern	3/4	♩	♩	♩	♩	♩	♩
underlying beat		—	—	—	—	—	—

Pas de Basque

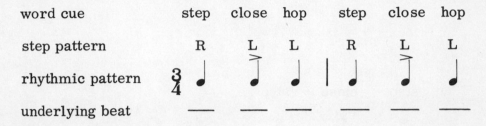

word cue		leap	step	close	leap	step	close
step pattern		Side R	Fwd. L	Fwd. R	Side R	Fwd. L	Fwd. R
rhythmic pattern	3/4 ... 2/4	♩	♩	♩	♩	♩	♩
underlying beat		—	—	—	—	—	—

Polka

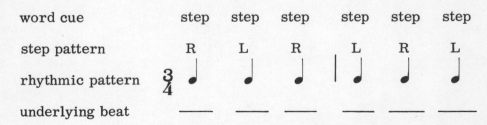

word cue		hop	step	close	step	hop	step	close	step	hop
step pattern		L	R	L	R	R	L	R	L	L
rhythmic pattern	2/4	♪	♪	♪	♪.	♪	♪	♪	♪.	♪
underlying beat			—		—	—		—	—	

Running Waltz

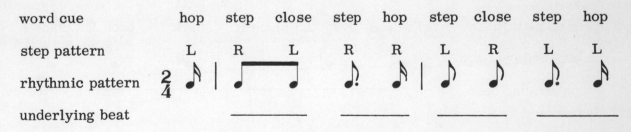

word cue		step	step	step	step	step	step
step pattern		R	L	R	L	R	L
rhythmic pattern	3/4	♩	♩	♩	♩	♩	♩
underlying beat		—	—	—	—	—	—

Schottische

	word cue	step	step	step	hop
	step pattern	R	L	R	R
	rhythmic pattern				
	underlying beat	──	──	──	──

Two–Step

	word cue	step	close	step
	step pattern	R	L	R
	rhythmic pattern			
	underlying beat	───────		───

Two–Step Balance

	word cue	step	toe	step	step	toe	step
	step pattern	Fwd. R	Fwd. L	place R	back L	back R	place L
	rhythmic pattern						
	underlying beat	────────────		────	────────		────

Waltz

	word cue	step	step	close	step	step	close
step pattern		Fwd. L	side R	side L	back R	side L	side R

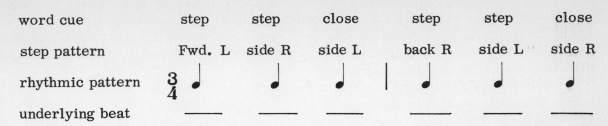

rhythmic pattern

underlying beat

Hop Waltz (turn)

	word cue	step	hop	step	hop
step pattern		Side L	half-turn clockwise	Side R	half-turn clockwise

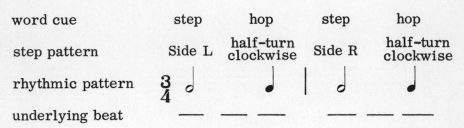

rhythmic pattern

underlying beat

Waltz Balance

	word cue	step	toe	step	step	toe	step
step pattern		Fwd. R	Fwd. L	place R	back L	back R	place L

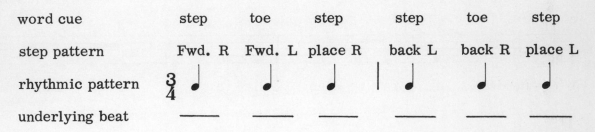

rhythmic pattern

underlying beat

Two Middle Eastern Folk Dances: Hora and Dubka. Folk dancing in Mediterranean countries is usually done in groups which move in open circles or lines. There is a leader who determines any changes in direction or step pattern. The two dances below are similar in that the group forms a semi-circle with arms linked at shoulder level or hands held down at the sides. There should be little movement from the waist up and the entire torso should follow the movement direction of the feet.

It is important to maintain an informal group spirit of gaiety and fun when doing these dances. Once the basic beat pattern is felt by the group, leaders should be encouraged to create other step patterns as they go along.

The following songs represent typical tunes used with each dance. There are numerous folk dance recordings which can also be used. (See Appendix E for suggestions).

Hava Nagila

Hava Nagila

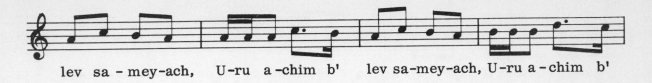

lev sa – mey-ach, U-ru a –chim b' lev sa-mey-ach, U-ru a –chim b'

lev sa – mey – ach U-ru a –chim b' – lev sa – mey –ach

U –ru a – chim, U –ru a –chim b'lev sa–mey – ach.

Dance Directions: 8-Beat Hora (Israeli)

Beat:	1	2	3	4	5	6	7	8
Foot:	R	L	R	R	L	L	L	L
Movement:	Step to R	Step to R behind R	Step to R	Hop	Step to L	Step to L behind L	Step to L	Hop

Ala Da'lona

(6—beat Dubka)

LEBANESE

A - la da' lo - na A - la da' lo - na

hi - war shi - ma - li gha - yar ih - lo - na

ma - ba - di i - mi ma - ba - di ba - yi

ba - di ha - bi - bi as - mar ih - lo - na.

Fair Da'lona with dark skin
Chilled by the wind; I would

leave my mother and father
to visit my fair Da'lona.

Dance Directions: 6-beat Dubka (Lebanese)

Beat:	1	2	3	4	5	6
Foot:	L	R	L	L	L	R
Movement:	Forward	Back	Forward	Back	Hop as R crosses in front of L ankle	Step to R

8-beat Dubka: The eight-beat Dubka is also very common and the music is found on many recordings of Middle Eastern folk dance music.[4] See catalog (sent upon request) of Rashid Record Company, Atlantic Ave., Brooklyn, New York.

Beat:	1	2	3	4	5	6	7	8
Foot:	L	R	L	R	L	L	L	R
Movement:	Forward	Back	Forward	Back	Forward	Back	Hop as R crosses in front of L ankle	Step to R

4. Several selections on this recording are also suitable acompaniment for the Hora.

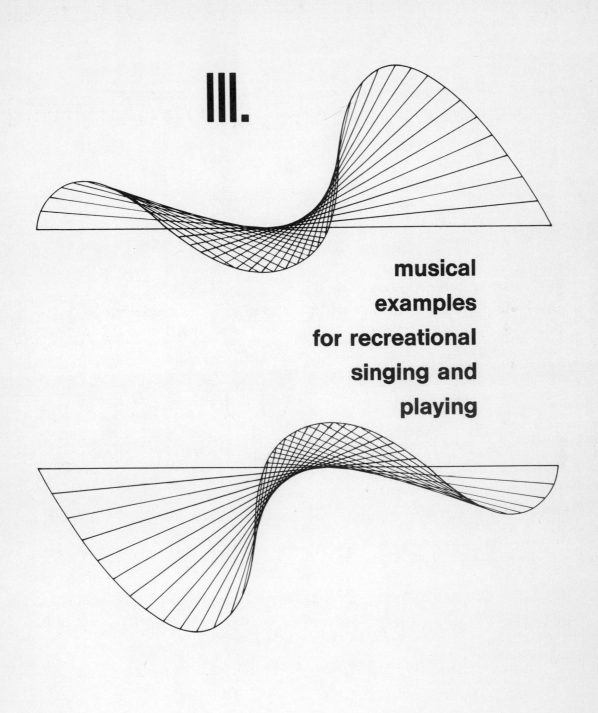

III.

musical
examples
for recreational
singing and
playing

America the Beautiful

KATHARINE LEE BATES

SAMUEL A. WARD

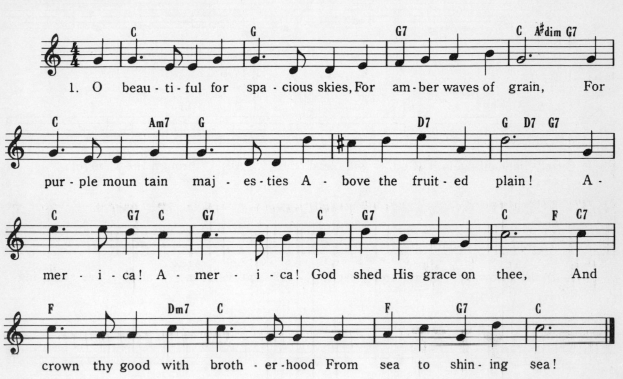

1. O beau-ti-ful for spa-cious skies, For am-ber waves of grain, For pur-ple moun tain maj-es-ties A-bove the fruit-ed plain! A-mer-i-ca! A-mer-i-ca! God shed His grace on thee, And crown thy good with broth-er-hood From sea to shin-ing sea!

2. O beautiful for Pilgrim feet,
Whose stern impassioned stress
A thoroughfare for freedom beat
Across the wilderness.
America! America! God mend thine every
    flaw,
Confirm thy soul in self-control,
Thy liberty in law.

3. O beautiful for heroes proved
In liberating strife,
Who more than self their country loved,
And mercy more than life.
America! America! May God thy gold refine
Till all success be nobleness
And every gain divine.

4. O beautiful for patriot dream
That sees beyond the years,
Thine alabaster cities gleam
Undimmed by human tears.
America! America! God shed His grace on thee,
And crown thy good with brotherhood
From sea to shining sea.

All Through the Night

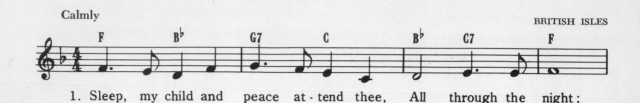

Calmly

BRITISH ISLES

F   B♭   G7   C   B♭   C7   F

1. Sleep, my child and peace at-tend thee, All through the night;

B♭   G7   C   B♭   C7   F

Guard-ian an-gels God will send thee, All through the night;

C7

Soft the drow-sy hours are creep-ing, Hill and vale in slum-ber steep-ing;

F   B♭   G7   C   B♭   C7   F

I my lov-ing vig-il keep-ing, All through the night.

2. While the moon her watch is keeping
   All through the night;
   While the heavy world is sleeping
   All through the night;
   O'er thy spirit gently stealing,
   Visions of delight revealing,
   Breathes a pure and holy feeling
   All through the night.

1. Holl amrantaur sêr ddywedant, Ar hyd y nos,
   "Dyma'r ffordd i fro gogoniant," Ar hyd y nos.
   Golen arall yw tywyllwch, I arddaug os gwir brydferthweh,
   Teulu'r nef oedd mewn tawelwch, Ar hyd y nos.

Buffalo Gals

(THREE LITTLE GIRLS)

With Animation

COOL WHITE

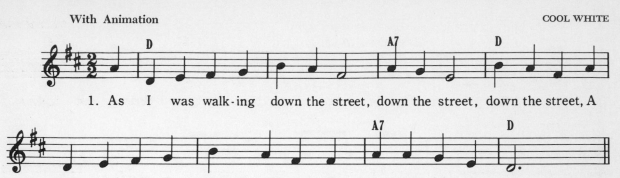

1. As I was walk-ing down the street, down the street, down the street, A

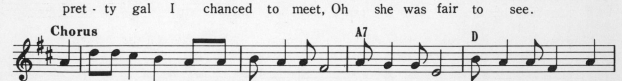

pret-ty gal I chanced to meet, Oh she was fair to see.

Oh, Buf-fa-lo Gals won't you come out to-night, come out to-night, come out to-night? Oh,

Buf-fa-lo Gals won't you come out to-night, and dance by the light of the moon?

2. I asked her if she'd stop and talk, stop and talk, stop and talk,
Her feet took up the whole sidewalk, and left no room for me.
3. I asked her if she'd be my wife, be my wife, be my wife,
Then I'd be happy all my life, if she'd marry me.

Blow the Man Down

Rapidly

CHANTEY

1. I'll sing you a song, a good song of the sea,

Way, hey, blow the man down; And

trust that you'll join in the cho-rus with me.

Give me some time to blow the man down.

Blow Ye Winds

Shoo, Fly, Don't Bother Me

Shoo, Fly, Don't Bother Me

1. I feel, I feel, I feel, I feel like a morn-ing star, I
feel, I feel, I feel, I feel like a morn-ing star.

2. I feel, I feel, I feel, I feel, like my mother said,
Like angels pouring 'lasses down on my little head.

Eency, Weency Spider

ACTION SONG

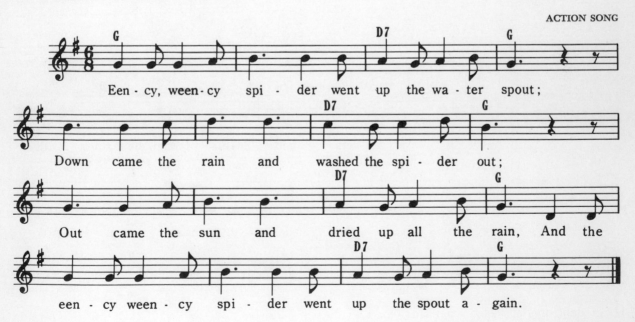

Een-cy, ween-cy spi-der went up the wa-ter spout;
Down came the rain and washed the spi-der out;
Out came the sun and dried up all the rain, And the
een-cy ween-cy spi-der went up the spout a-gain.

Yankee Doodle

U. S.

1. O fath'r and I went down to camp, a - long with Cap-tain Good' - in, And
there we saw the men and boys as thick as hast - y pud - din.'

Chorus

Yan - kee Doo-dle keep it up, Yan - kee Doo - dle Dan - dy,
Mind the mu - sic and the step, And with the girls be hand - y.

La Raspe

TR. MAURICE TALBOT

MEXICO

With click-ing of cas - ta - nets and jin-gle of tam - bou - rine, All
work of the day for - got, and danc-ing to - night is queen. We're
danc-ing a dance from old Mex - i - co, La la la la la la; Our
steps light and gay, and our hearts a - glow, La la la la la la.

Frog Went Courting

KENTUCKY

1. Frog went court-ing, he did ride, Rink-tum bod-dy mitch-a - cam - bo.

Sword and buck-ler by his side, Rink-tum bod-dy mitch-a - cam - bo.

Chorus

Kim - an - i - ro, down to Cai - ro, Kim - an - i - ro,

Cai - ro; Strad - a - lad - da - lad - a - bod - dy,

Lad - da - bod- dy - link - tum, Rink - tum bod- dy mitch-a - cam - bo.

2. To the lady mouse said he, "Will you kindly marry me?" etc.
3. Who can make the wedding gown? Old Miss Rat from London town, etc.
4. Then there came a big Tom Cat. So long frog and mouse and rat! etc.

Finlandia

SALLY MONSOUR AND JOHN BATCHELLER

JEAN SIBELIUS

1. God grant us peace and depth of under stand-ing,____
____ That we may live and share the world as one. ____
____ With joy and love we seek all men as brothers, ____
____ And come to feel the free-dom just be-gun. ____
____ As brothers all we share this world to-geth er, ____
____ And light the can - dle of our ris ing sun. ____

2. Through storm and stress thy heroes shall not fail thee,
   Though perils press them hard on every hand;
   God grant them strength and courage when the need be,
   Clear eyes to see, and hearts to understand.
   God lead thee on through nobleness to triumph,
   God make thee great, my own native land.

Every Time I Feel the Spirit

SPIRITUAL

Eve-ry time I___ feel the spir-it___ mov-ing in my heart___ I will pray. Eve-ry time I___ feel the spir-it___ mov-ing in my heart___ I will pray.

Verse

1. Up-on the moun-tain___ when my Lord spoke, Out of His mouth came___ fire and smoke. Up-on the moun-tain___ when my Lord spoke, Out of His mouth came___ fire and smoke.

2. Looked all around me, it sure looked fine;
   I asked my Lord if it were mine.
   Looked all around me, it sure looked fine;
   I asked my Lord if it were mine.

We Wish You a Merry Christmas

2. Please bring us some figgy pudding, please bring us some figgy pudding,
   Please bring us some figgy pudding, please bring it right here.

3. We won't leave until we get some, we won't leave until we get some,
   We won't leave until we get some, please bring it right here.

At the Gate of Heaven
(A LA PUERTO DEL CIELO)

DR. A. D. ZANZIG

SPAIN

1. At the gate of heav'n lit - tle shoes they are sell - ing

For the lit - tle bare - foot - ed an - gels there dwell - ing.

Slum - ber, my ba - by, slum - ber my ba - by,

Slum - ber, my ba - by, a - rru, a - rru.

2. God will bless the children so peacefully sleeping,
God will help the mothers whose love they are keeping.

1. A la puerto del cielo Venden zapatos,
Para los angelitos que endan descalzos,
Duermete, niño, duermete, niño,
Duermete, niño, arru, arru.

2. A los niños que duermen Dios los bendice,
A las madres que velan Dios las asiste,
Duermete, niño, duermete, niño,
Duermete, niño, arru, arru.

Every Night When the Sun Goes Down

1. Oh, ev - 'ry - night _____ when the sun goes down, _____
_____ Oh, ev - 'ry - night _____ when the sun goes down, _____
_____ Oh, ev - 'ry night _____ when the sun goes down, _____
_____ I hang down my head _____ and mourn-ful cry. _____

2. True love, don't weep, true love don't mourn, (three times)
   I'm going away from this old town.

3. Oh, how I wish that train would come, (three times)
   To take me back to where I'm from.

4. And when that train does finally come, (three times)
   I'm going back to my old home.

5. Oh, how I wish my babe was born,
   And sitting on his daddy's knee,
   And I, poor girl, was dead and gone,
   With green grass growing over me.

6. My love is gone, where can he be? (three times)
   He no longer gives his love to me.

7. True love, don't weep, true love don't mourn, (three times)
   I'm going away from this old town.

New River Train

1. I'm rid-in' on that new riv-er train,———— I'm rid-in' on that new riv-er train;———— The same old train that brought me here's gon-na car-ry me home a-gain.————

2. Darling, you can't love two, (twice)
   You can't love two, and still to me be true, (etc.)

3. Darling, you can't love three, (twice)
   You can't love three, and still be true to me, (etc.)

4. Darling, you can't love four, (twice)
   You can't love four, and love me any more, (etc.)

5. Darling, you can't love five, (twice)
   You can't love five, and have my love survive, (etc.)

6. Darling, you can't love six, (twice)
   You can't love six, and do those tricks, (etc.)

7. Darling, you can't love seven, (twice)
   You can't love seven, and ever get to heaven, (etc.)

8. Darling, you can't love eight, (twice)
   You can't love eight, and pass the Pearly Gate, (etc.)

9. Darling, you can't love nine, (twice)
   You can't love nine, and still be mine, (etc.)
   (repeat the first verse)

O Hanukkah

SALLY MONSOUR AND JOHN BATCHELLER

JEWISH FOLK SONG

O Ha-nuk-kah, O Ha-nuk-kah, We greet you with danc-ing,,

This is the time to be gay and ro-manc-ing, come and sing the song of re-

joic-ing and peace, Ha-nuk-kah is here may our joys never cease, And

While we are danc-ing, the can-dles are burn-ing bright.

One for each day we will light on our way, Re-

joic-ing with hearts that are light,   joic-ing with hearts that are light.

Wondrous Love

SOUTHERN U. S.

1. What won-drous love is this, O my soul, O my soul! What won-drous love is this, O my soul!_____ What won-drous love is this that caused the Lord_ of bliss To send this bless-ed gift for my soul, for my soul, To send this bless-ed gift for my soul:_____

2. When I was sinking down, sinking down, sinking down,
   When I was sinking down, sinking down;
   When I was sinking down beneath God's righteous frown,
   Christ laid aside His crown for my soul, for my soul,
   Christ laid aside His crown for my soul.

3. And when from death I'm free, I'll sing on, I'll sing on,
   And when from death I'm free, I'll sing on;
   And when from death I'm free, I'll sing and joyful be,
   And through eternity I'll sing on, I'll sing on,
   And through eternity I'll sing on.

Loch Lomond

SCOTLAND

1. By___ yon bon-nie banks and by yon bon-nie braes, Where the sun shines bright on Loch Lo - mond, Where me and my true love were ev-er wont to gae, On the bon-nie, bon-nie banks of Loch Lo - mond.

Chorus

Oh! ye'll take the high road, and I'll take the low road, And I'll be in Scot - land a - fore ye, But me and my true love we'll nev-er meet a - gain On the bon-nie, bon-nie banks of Loch Lo - mond.

2. 'Twas there that we parted in yon shady glen
On the steep, steep side of Ben Lomond,
Where in purple hue the highland hills we view,
And the moon coming out in the gloaming.

3. The wee birdies sing, and the wild flowers spring,
And in sunshine the waters are sleeping,
But the broken hearts kens nae second spring again,
Though the waeful may cease frae their greeting.

Beautiful Homeland

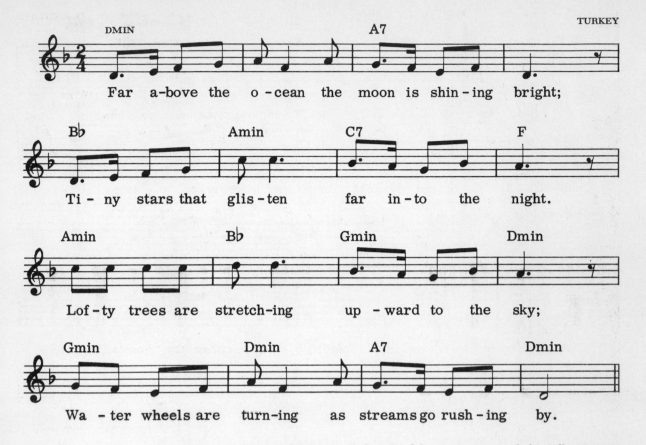

TURKEY

Far a-bove the o-cean the moon is shin-ing bright;

Ti-ny stars that glis-ten far in-to the night.

Lof-ty trees are stretch-ing up-ward to the sky;

Wa-ter wheels are turn-ing as streams go rush-ing by.

—Melody by Ali Ulvi Baradan, Izmir, Turkey. Used by permission. words by Sally Monsour

One More River

(NOAH'S ARK)

SPIRITUAL

1. Old No-ah built him-self an ark, There's one more riv-er to cross, And built it all of hick-o-ry bark, There's one more riv-er to cross.

Chorus

One more riv-er,____ And that's the riv-er of Jor-dan; One more riv-er,____ There's one more riv-er to cross.____

2. The animals came two by two, there's one more river to cross,
   The elephant and kangaroo, there's one more river to cross.

3. The animals came three by three, there's one more river to cross,
   The baboon and the chimpanzee, there's one more river to cross.

4. The animals came four by four, there's one more river to cross,
   Old Noah got mad and hollered for more, there's one more river to cross.

5. The animals came five by five, there's one more river to cross,
   The bees came swarming from the hive, there's one more river to cross.

6. The animals came six by six, there's one more river to cross,
   The lion laughed at the monkey's tricks, there's one more river to cross.

7. When Noah found he had no sail, there's one more river to cross,
   He just ran up his old coat tail, there's one more river to cross.

8. Before the voyage did begin, there's one more river to cross.
   Old Noah pulled the gangplank in, there's one more river to cross.

9. They never knew where they were at, there's one more river to cross,
   'Til the old ark bumped on Ararat, there's one more river to cross.

Lone Star Trail

U. S. COWBOY

1. I start-ed on the trail on June twen-ty-third, I've been
punch-ing Tex-as cat-tle on the Lone Star Trail;

Chorus

Sing-ing ki - yi yip - pi yap - pi yay, yap-pi yay! Sing-ing
ki - yi yip - pi yap - pi yay._____

2. I'm up in the morning long before daylight,
   And before I'm sleeping the moon is shining bright, etc.

3. My feet are in the stirrups and my rope is at my side,
   And I never yet have seen the horse that I can't ride, etc.

4. Oh, it's bacon and beans about every day,
   And I'd just about as soon be eating prairie hay, etc.

5. Now my seat is in the saddle, and my hand is on my rope,
   And my eye is on the dogies, I'm a good cow poke, etc.

6. With my knees in the saddle and my seat in the sky,
   I'll continue punching cattle in the sweet by and by, etc.

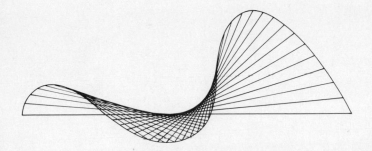 **appendices**

APPENDIX A

General Sources on Recreation and Leisure

A Guide to Books in Recreation. 14th annual edition. Washington, D. C.: National Recreation and Park Association, 1971.

ARTZ, ROBERT M. *Quest for United Action for Recreation.* Available from National Recreation and Park Association, 1970.

CARLSON, REYNOLD E.; DEPPE, THEODORE R.; and MACLEAN, JANET R. *Recreation in American Life.* Belmont, Calif.: Wadsworth, 1963.

College and University Facilities Guide for Health, Physical Education, Recreation, and Athletics. 4th Annual National Facilities Conference, 1968. Available from National Recreation and Park Association, Washington, D. C.

CORBIN, H. DEN. *Recreation Leadership.* 3rd ed. Englewood Cliffs, N. J.: Prentice-Hall, Inc., 1970.

DULLES, FOSTER RHEA. *A History of Recreation.* New York: Appleton, Century Crofts, 1965.

Employment Outlook for Recreation Workers. Bulletin No. 1650-43. Washington, D. C.: U. S. Department of Labor, 1970.

Evaluation of Park and Recreation Agencies. Washington, D. C.: National Recreation and Park Association.

Journal of Leisure Research. Published annually by the National Recreation and Park Association, Washington, D. C.

KRAUS, RICHARD. *Recreation Today: Program Planning and Leadership.* New York: Macmillan Co., 1964.

MADOW, PAULINE. *Recreation in America.* New York: H. W. Wilson Co., 1965.

MEYER, HAROLD; BRIGHTBILL, CHARLES K.; and SESSOMS, H. DOUGLAS. *Community Recreation: A Guide to Its Organization.* rev. New York: A. S. Barnes, 1950.

———. and BRIGHTBILL, CHARLES K. *Recreation Administration: A Guide to Its Practices.* Englewood Cliffs, New Jersey: Prentice-Hall, 1956.

MUSSELMAN, VIRGINIA, and FRIESWYK, SIEBOLT H. *Music Is Recreation.* Available from National Recreation and Park Association, Washington, D. C.

———. *Guidelines for the Organization and Administration of a Cultural Program in Community Recreation.* New York: Assoc. Press, n.d.

NEUMEYER, MARTIN, and NEUMEYER, ESTHER. *A Study of Leisure and Recreation in Their Sociological Aspects.* New York: Ronald Press, 1955.

Recreation Research. Compiled by American Association for Health, Physical Education and Recreation, and National Recreation and Park Association. Washington, D. C.: National Recreation and Park Association, 1965.

ROTONNO, ARNOLD. "A Statistical Study to Examine the Amount of Knowledge Effected by Recreation Experiences in Music." Unpublished master's thesis, University of Illinois, 1961.

VANNIER, MARYHELEN. *Methods and Materials in Recreation Leadership.* Philadelphia, Pa.: Saunders, 1960.

Basic Sources and References on the Teaching of Music

I. Books on the Teaching of Music.

Textbooks, recent or recently revised, which offer both the theory and practice of music teaching for children of elementary school age. All sources are current—numerous additional references are also available.

ARONOFF, FRANCES WEBBER. *Music and Young Children.* New York: Holt, Rinehart, and Winston, Inc., 1969.

BERGETHON, BJORNER, and BOARDMAN, EUNICE. *Musical Growth in the Elementary School.* New York: Holt, Rinehart, and Winston, Inc., rev., 1970.

CHEYETTE, R. PHYLLIS, and CHEYETTE, HERBERT. *Teaching Music Creatively in the Elementary School.* New York: McGraw-Hill, 1969.

GELINEAU, R. PHILLIS. *Experiences in Music.* New York: McGraw-Hill Inc., 1970.

GREEN, ELIZABETH. *The Modern Conductor.* Englewood Cliffs, N. J.: Prentice-Hall, 1961.

HARTSHORN, WILLIAM. *Music for the Academically Talented Student in the Secondary School.* Washington, D. C.: National Education Association, 1960.

HOFFER, CHARLES. *Teaching Music in the Secondary Schools.* Belmont, Calif.: Wadsworth Pub. Co., 1965.

MARSH, MARY VAL. *Explore and Discover Music.* New York: Macmillan Co., 1970.

NYE, ROBERT E., and NYE, VERNICE T. *Music in the Elementary School.* 3rd ed., Englewood Cliffs, New Jersey: Prentice-Hall Inc., 1970.

RAEBECK, LOIS, and WHEELER, LAWRENCE. *New Approaches to Music in the Elementary School.* Dubuque, Iowa: Wm. C. Brown Company Publishers, 1969.

SCHAEFFER, MURRAY. *When Words Sing.* New York: Associated Music Pub., 1970.

SUR, WILLIAM, and SCHULLER, CHARLES. *Music Education for Teenagers.* 2nd ed. New York: Harper and Row, 1966.

SWANSON, BESSIE. *Music in the Education of Children.* Belmont, Calif.: Wadsworth Pub. Co., 1969.

WILSON, VERNE. *Design for Musical Understanding.* Evanston, Ill.: Summy-Birchard, 1966.

II. Basic Series

Textbooks for school use in Kindergarten through Grade 9. Each series includes student books, teachers editions, and recordings. Details about the underlying philosophy and the particular emphasis of each series are available from the publisher.

Birchard Music Series, Summy-Birchard Co., 1959-62.
Discovering Music Together, Follett Pub. Co., 1966, rev., 1969.
Exploring Music, Holt, Rinehart, and Winston, Inc., 1965-69, rev. 1971.
Growing with Music, Prentice-Hall, Inc., 1963-66.
Making Music Your Own, Silver-Burdett Co., 1964-69.
New Dimensions in Music, American Book Co., 1970.
The Magic of Music, Ginn and Co., 1965-69.
This Is Music, Allyn and Bacon, Inc., 1962-65, rev. 1967-68.

III. Special Resources

All companies will promptly supply catalogs with annotations of their materials.

Adventures In Music. (Tipton), RCA Records, New York.

A graded series of twelve albums, with accompanying manual, containing numerous selections of fine music. Each volume available separately.

Bowmar Record and Publishing Co., 622 Rodier Dr., Glendale, Calif. 91209.

Filmstrips, records, and books of folk music from different parts of the world presented in simple, authentic form. Noteworthy are songs and activities for children with special needs.

Cooperative Recreation Service, Inc., Radnor Rd., Delaware, Ohio 43015.

Folk song and dance collections. Classified and available in suitable subject headings. Especially good for all types of community singing, recreational and camping use. Small, pocket-sized editions available.

Folkways/Scholastic, 906 Sylvan Ave., Englewood Cliffs, New Jersey 07632.

Valuable source for ethnic music of the world's people including an excellent selection of folk music of the Americas.

Keynote Music Service, Inc. 833 South Olive St., Los Angeles, Calif. 90052.

An efficient distribution service with classified listings of music for centralized ordering purposes. Listings available upon request.

National Center for Audio-Tapes, Audio-Visual Department, University of Colorado, Boulder, Colorado.

Duplicates of thousands of audio-tapes available at a small fee. Catalog listing includes foreign taped interviews, educational broadcasts, etc.

National Record Plan, 28 West 25th St., New York, New York 10001.

Supplies educational institutions and libraries with discounts on recordings as listed in the Schwann Catalog and tapes as listed in the Harrison Tape catalog.

Our Heritage of American Folk Music and *Our Heritage of American Patriotic Music.*

Two sets of filmstrips with related pictures, songs, and captions; both educational and inspirational.

Society for Visual Education, 1345 W. Diversey Pky., Chicago, Ill. 60607.

Time-Life History of the United States, Silver-Burdett Co., Morristown, New Jersey 01960.

Literature, historical documents, speeches, and music of each era in U. S. history. Several volumes.

World Library of Folk and Primitive Music, Columbia Records, New York.

A multi-volume series of authentic music of primitive and folk origin from all corners of the world.

Selected Books About Music for
Libraries and Recreation Centers

I. For Young People

The following books are generally suited for young readers in pre-teen and early-teen years.

ANDERSON, MARIAN. *My Lord, What a Morning.* New York: Viking, 1956.

APEL, WILLI, and DANIEL, RALPH. *The Harvard Brief Dictionary of Music.* Cambridge, Mass.: Harvard University Press, 1960.

ATTAWAY, WILLIAM. *Hear America Singing.* Introduction by Harry Belafonte. New York: Lion, 1968.

BAKELESS, KATHERINE L. *Story Lives of Great Composers.* rev. Philadelphia: Lippincott, 1953.

BALET, JAN. *What Makes an Orchestra.* New York: Oxford, 1951.

BALLIETT, WHITNEY. *Dinosaurs in the Morning.* Philadelphia: J. B. Lippincott, Co., 1962. Description of Jazz.

BERNSTEIN, LEONARD. *The Joy of Music.* New York: Simon and Schuster, 1959.

———. *Young Peoples Concerts for Reading and Listening.* New York: Simon and Schuster, 1962. (Book and five 7 inch 33 1/3 recordings.)

BERNSTEIN, SHIRLEY. *Making Music:* Leonard Bernstein. Chicago: Encyclopedia Brittanica, 1963.

BRAND, OSCAR. *Singing Holidays.* New York: Knopf, 1957.

BRITTEN, BENJAMIN, and HOLST, IMOGEN. *Wonderful World of Music.* Garden City, New York: David McKay Co., Inc., rev. 1969.

BROWNE, CHARLES, A. rev. by Willard Heaps, *The Story of Our National Ballads.* New York: Crowell, 1960.

BUCHANAN, FANNIE, and LUCKENBILL, CHARLES. *How Man Made Music.* rev. Chicago: Follett, 1959.

BULLA, CLYDE. *Stories of Favorite Operas.* New York: Crowell, 1959.

BURCH, GLADYS. *Famous Pianists for Boys and Girls.* New York: Dodd, Mead, 1956.

———. *Famous Violinists for Young People.* New York: Dodd, Mead, 1946.

CHISSELL, JOAN. *Chopin.* New York: Crowell, 1965.

CROSS, MILTON. *New Complete Stories of Great Operas.* rev. New York: Doubleday, 1955.

CROSS, MILTON, and EWEN, JOHN and DAVID. *Encyclopedia of the Great Composers and Their Music.* rev. New York: Doubleday, 1962.

CUNNINGHAM, DALE. *Picture Book of Music and Its Makers.* New York: Sterling, 1963.

DAVIS, MARILYN, and BROIDO, ARNOLD. *Music Dictionary.* rev. New York: Doubleday, 1956.

CRAIG, JEAN. *The Story of Musical Notes.* New York: Lerner Pub., 1962.

DEITZ, BETTY, and OLATUNJI, MICHAEL. *Musical Instruments of Africa,* (with 7 inch record). New York: John Day, 1965.

EATON, JEANETTE. *Trumpeter's Tale.* New York: Morrow, 1955. (The Story of Louis Armstrong.)

ERLICH, LILLIAN. *What Is Jazz All About?* New York: Messner, 1962.

EWEN, DAVID. *Encyclopedia of Concert Music.* New York: Hill and Wang, 1959.

———. *The Story of Jerome Kern.* New York: Holt, 1953.

———. *The Story of Arturo Toscanini.* rev. New York: Holt, 1960.

———. *A Journey into Greatness: The Life and Music of George Gershwin.* New York: Holt, 1956.

———. *The Story of Irving Berlin.* New York: Holt, 1950.

———. *The World of Jerome Kern.* New York: Holt, 1960.

———. *Famous Instrumentalists.* New York: Dodd, Mead, 1965.

————, BERNSTEIN, LEONARD. *A Biography for Young People.* Philadelphia: Chilton, 1965.
FOX, LILLA M. *Instruments of Popular Music.* New York: Roy, 1968.
FROST, FRANCES. *Amahl and the Night Visitors.* New York: McGraw-Hill Book Co., Inc., 1952.
GOLLOMB, JOSEPH. *Albert Schweitzer, Genius of the Jungle.* New York: Vanguard, 1949.
GOUGH, CATHERINE. *Boyhoods of Great Composers.* Books 1 and 2. New York: Walck, 1961, 1965.
HENTOFF, NAT. *Jazz Country.* New York: Harper & Row, 1965.
HIGGINS, HELEN. *Stephen Foster, Boy Minstrel.* Indianapolis: Bobbs, Merrill, 1953.
HUGHES, LANGSTON. *Famous Negro Music Makers.* New York: Dodd, Mead, 1955.
————. *First Book of Jazz.* New York: Watts, 1955.
HYATT, MALCOLM and FABELL, WALTER. comp., *Gilbert and Sullivan Song Book.* New York: Random House, 1955.
IRVING, ROBERT. *Sound and Ultrasonics.* New York: Knopf, 1959.
KAUFFMAN, HELEN L. *The Story of Haydn.* New York: Grossett and Dunlap, 1962.
KEEPNEWS, ORRIN, and GRAUER, BILL. *Pictorial History of Jazz.* New York: Crown, 1955.
KELLOGG, CHARLOTTE H. *Paderewski.* New York: Viking, 1956.
KERT, RUSSELL, and TAYLOR, DEEMS. Compiled by Rupert Hughes. *Music Lovers' Encyclopedia.* New York: Garden City, 1954.
LERNER, SHARON. *Places of Musical Fame.* Minneapolis, Minn.: Lerner Pub., 1967.
LINGG, ANN M. *John Philip Sousa.* New York: Holt, 1954.

MACHLIS, JOSEPH. *American Composers of Our Time.* New York: Crowell, 1963.
MAYNARD, OLGA. *The Ballet Companion.* Philadelphia: Macrae Smith, 1957.
McGEHEE, THOMASINE, and NELSON, ALICE. *People and Music.* Boston: Allyn and Bacon, Inc., 1963.
MIRSKY, REBA PAEFF. *Johann Sebastian Bach.* Chicago: Follett, 1965.
————. *Beethoven.* Chicago: Follett, 1957.
————. *Haydn.* Chicago: Follett, 1963.
————. *Mozart.* Chicago: Follett, 1960.
PAULI, HERTHA. *Silent Night, The Story of a Song.* New York: Knopf, 1951.
POSELL, ELSA. *American Composers.* Boston: Houghton Mifflin, 1963.
————. *This Is an Orchestra.* Boston: Houghton Mifflin, 1950. (Story about the orchestra.)
POWER-WATERS, ALMA S. *Melody Maker.* New York: Dutton, 1959. (The life of Sir Arthur Sullivan.)
RUBLONSKY, JOHN. *Popular Music.* New York: Basic Books, Inc., 1967.
SIEGMEISTER, ELIE. *Invitation to Music.* Irvington-on-Hudson, New York: Harvey House, 1961. (Record—Invitation to Music, Folkways FT 3603.)
SHIPPEN, KATHERINE, and SEIDLOVA, ANCA. *The Heritage of Music.* New York: Viking, 1963.
SLONIMSKY, NICHOLAS. *The Road to Music.* rev. New York: Dodd, Mead, 1966.
STAMBLER, IRWIN. *The Worlds of Sound.* New York: W. W. Norton. 1967.
STODDARD, HOPE. *From These Come Music.* New York: Crowell, 1962.
TERKEL, STUDS. *Giants of Jazz.* New York: Crowell, 1957.
THOMAS, HENRY, and THOMAS, DANA LEE. *Living Biographies of Great Composers.* New York: 1959.
TRAPP, MARIA. *The Story of the Trapp Family Singers.* Philadelphia: Lippincott, 1949.
ULANOV, BARRY. *Handbook of Jazz.* New York: Viking, 1957.
ULRICH, HOMER. *Famous Women Singers.* New York: Dodd, Mead, 1956.

II. For Adults

The following books are suitable for adult reading and reference. The list is highly selective.

ANDERSON, MARIAN. *My Lord, What a Morning.* New York: Viking, 1958. (An autobiography.)
APEL, WILLI. *Harvard Brief Dictionary of Music.* Cambridge, Mass.: Harvard University Press, 1960.
ATTAWAY, WILLIAM. *Hear America Sing.* New York: Lion, 1968.
AYRE, LESLIE. ed. *The Wit of Music.* Boston: Crescendo Pub., 1966. (Cartoons and stories about composers and musicians.)
BARLOW, HOWARD, and MORGENSTERN, SAM. *A Dictionary of Musical Themes.* New York: Crown, Pub., 1948.
CARUSO, DOROTHY. *Enrico Caruso.* New York: Simon and Schuster, 1945.
CHOOTE, ROBERT, and ROSSI, NICK. *Music of Our Time.* Boston: Crescendo Pub., 1970.
COHN, NIK. *Rock from the Beginning.* New York: Stein and Day. 1969.
COPLAND, AARON. *What to Listen for in Music.* New York: McGraw-Hill, 1939.
CROSS, MILTON. *New Complete Stories of Great Operas.* rev. New York: Doubleday, 1955.
————, and EWEN, DAVID. *Encyclopedia of the Great Composers and Their Music.* rev. New York: Doubleday, 1962.
DAVIS, M. K. *Musical Dictionary.* New York: Doubleday, 1958.
EWEN, DAVID. *The Story of Arturo Toscanini.* New York: Holt, 1960.

———. *Complete Book of 20th Century Music.* Englewood Cliffs, N. J.: Prentice-Hall Inc., 1952.

———. *Famous Instrumentalists.* New York: Dodd, Mead, 1965.

———. *With a Song in His Heart.* New York: Holt, 1963. (Story of Richard Rodgers.)

HENTOFF, NAT. *Jazz Country.* New York: Harper and Row, 1965. (A must for those interested in Jazz.)

JAMES, BURNETT. *An Adventure in Music.* Boston: Crescendo Pub., n.d. (Simple adventure story about a man with polio and his experiences with music.)

JONES, LEROI. *Black Music.* New York: Willam Morrow. 1971.

MACHLIS, JOSEPH. *Introduction to Contemporary Music.* New York: W. W. Norton, 1961.

———. *Music Adventures in Listening.* New York: W. W. Norton, 1968.

MILLER, HUGH. *Introduction to Music Appreciation.* New York: Chilton Co., 1961.

NORDHOLM, HARRIET. *Birchard Opera Series Guides.* Evanston, Ill.: Summy-Birchard Co., 1965.

OLIVER, PAUL. *The Story of the Blues.* New York: Chilton Press. 1969.

ROREM, NED. *Music and People.* New York: George Braziller. 1968.

RUBLOWSKY, JOHN. *Black Music in America.* New York: Basic Books. 1971.

SHAW, ARNOLD, *The Rock Revolution.* London: Collier and Macmillan Ltd. 1969.

SOUTHERN, EILEEN, *The Music of Black Americans*: *A History*, New York: W. W. Norton. 1971.

THOMPSON, OSCAR. *How to Understand Music.* New York: Fawcett Pub., 1958.

ULANOV, BARRY. *Handbook of Jazz.* New York: Viking, 1957.

ULRICH, HOMER. *Famous Women Singers.* New York: Dodd, Mead, 1956.

Sources on Playing Instruments for Recreation

I. Books

BAY, MEL. *The Mel Bay Guitar Method*. Kirkwood, Mo.: Mel Bay Publ., 1960.

BECKMAN, FREDERICK. *Music for Melody Instruments*. Philadelphia: Elkan-Vogel Co., 1952.

BENTLEY, ARNOLD. *Songs to Sing and Play*. London: Novello and Co., 1964.

EDISON, ROGER. *Guitar Fun*. Westbury, L. I.: Pro-Art Pub., 1965.

EISENKRAMER, HENRY, *Strum and Sing*. Evanston, Ill., Summy-Birchard Co.

GILMORE, LEE. *Folk Instruments*. Minneapolis: Lerner Pub. Co., 1962.

GORNSTON, DAVID. *Your First 10 Recorder Lessons*. New York: Sam Fox Pub., n.d.

HALL, FRANCES. *How to Play the Autoharp*. Boston: The Boston Music Co., 1956.

HARVEY, ARTHUR. *How to Play the Recorder*.

HAWKINS, JOHN, and FAULHABER, MARTHA. *Music and Instruments for Children to Make*. New York: Albert Whitman Pub. Co., n.d.

Hobby Course for Piano. Dekalb, Ill.: Wurlitzer Co., 1970.

HOOD, MARGUERITE. *Teaching Rhythm and Using Classroom Instruments*. Englewood Cliffs, N. J.: Prentice-Hall, Inc., 1970.

KEEN, LAURA JOHNSON. *Sing and Play the Ukulele*. Far Rockaway, N.Y.: Carl Van Roy Co., 1957.

KRONE, BEATRICE P. *Harmony Fun with the Autoharp*. Park Ridge, Ill.: Neil A. Kjos Music Co., Pub., 1952.

LANG, TERRY. *Your First 10 Bass Guitar Lessons*. New York: Sam Fox Pub., n.d.

———. *Your First 10 Banjo Lessons*. New York: Sam Fox Pub., n.d.

LEE, RONNY. *Folk Strums for Guitar*. New York: Sam Fox Pub., n.d.

LUDWIG, ALICE J., and LUDWIG, LOUIS. *Colors and Chords*. Far Rockaway, N.Y.: Carl Van Roy Co.

McLAUGHLIN, R., and DAWLEY, MURIEL. *Sing and Play with the Autoharp*. Far Rockaway, N.Y.: Carl Van Roy Co., 1958.

———. *Make Music with Bells*. Far Rockaway, L I.: Carl Van Roy Co., 1958.

MONSOUR, SALLY, and NELSON M. J. *Play! (Piano Method for Older Beginners)*. New York: Marks Music Corp., 1963.

MOORE, JACK. *Music for the Guitar*. Chicago: M. M. Cole Pub., Co., 1962.

MOTTOLA, TONY. *Play the Guitar in 30 Minutes*. New York: Sam Fox Pub., Co., n.d.

PETERSON, MEG. *The Many Ways to Play the Autoharp*. Union, N. J.: Oscar Schmidt, Inc., 1968.

ROWEN, RUTH, and BILL SIMON. *Jolly Come Sing and Play*. New York: Carl Fischer, Inc., 1956.

SEDLON, J. H. *Play-a-Tune*. (Flutaphone, song Flute, or Tonette). New York: Sam Fox Pub., n.d.

SILVERMAN, JERRY. *Beginning the Folk Guitar*. New York: Oak Pub., Co., n.d.

SLAYMAN, HERMAN H. *American School for the Guitar*. Cincinnati, Ohio: Canyon Press: 1970.

SLIND, LLOYD H. *Melody, Rhythm, and Harmony for the Elementary Grades*. New York: Mills Music, Inc., 1953.

SNYDER, ALICE M. *Sing and Strum*. New York: Mills Music, Inc., 1957.

STAPLES, R. *Let's Play the Classroom Instruments*. Far Rockaway, N.Y.: Carl Van Roy Co., 1958.

SWIFT, FREDERIC FAY. *Together We Sing and Play*. New York: Edward B. Marks Music Corp., 1964.

TAUSSIG, HARRY. *Folk Style Guitar*. New York: Oak Pub. Co., 1967.

THURBAN, T. W. *How to Play the Harmonica*. New York: Sam Fox Pub., n.d.

TIMMERMAN, MAURINE, and GRIFFITH, CELESTE. *Guitar in the Classroom*. Dubuque, Iowa: Wm. C. Brown Company Publishers, 1971.

The Guitar in the Classroom. Chicago: Am. Music Conference, 1967.

II. Recordings

Beginner's 5-String Banjo. Chattanooga, Tenn., Don Sellers, Inc.

Beginner's Ukulele. Chattanooga, Tenn., Don Sellers, Inc.

Beginning the Folk Guitar. 1 12″ LP (LCR-64-1584), Folkways Records #8353.

Complete Autoharp. Walter Duda, Chattanooga, Tenn., Don Sellers, Inc.

Country and Folk Guitar, (Recording and Charts). Chattanooga, Tenn., Don Sellers, Inc.

The Folksinger's Guitar Guide, vols. 1 and 2. 2 12″ LP's (LCR-65-948), Folkways Records #8354 and 8356.

Strum for Fun, (Book, charts, and recording), Chattanooga, Tenn., Don Sellers, Inc.

Tuning Your Autoharp with Meg Peterson. Union, New Jersey. Oscar Schmidt Co. Gives instructions and includes sounds.

APPENDIX E

Sources on Rhythms, Movement, and Dancing

I. Books

ANDREWS, GLADYS. *Creative Rhythmic Movement for Children*. Englewood Cliffs, New Jersey: Prentice-Hall, Inc., 1954.

Everything the title implies. Excellent summary of the periods of child development and their impact on creative movement. Includes suggestions for making percussion instruments.

BAUER, LOIS, and REED, BARBARA. *Dance and Play Activities for the Elementary Grades*. 2 vols. New York: Chartwell House, Inc., 1953-54.

Activities for rhythmic response. Vol. 1 is for grades 1-3 and vol. 2 for grades 4-6.

BURGER, ISABEL. *Creative Play Acting*. New York: A. S. Barnes & Co., 1950.

Many interesting teaching ideas. Especially suited to primary grades.

COHEN, MARILYN; LINDELL, PATRICIA; and MONSOUR, SALLY. *Rhythm in Music and Dance for Children*. Belmont, California: Wadsworth Publishing Co., 1966.

Teaching ideas and lesson plans for rhythms and movement.

DOLL, EDNA, and NELSON, MARY JARMAN. *Rhythms Today*. Morristown, New Jersey: Silver Burdett Co., 1964.

Imaginative and comprehensive. Especially good for teachers who wish to integrate rhythmic movement and dance with music. Recordings available to accompany lessons in the book.

DRIVER, ANN. *Music and Movement*. London, New York: Oxford University Press, 1943.

Probably the classic book in the field—creative and practical. Still used extensively; reprinted six times since its publication. Of special value is the excellent chapter on music and movement for boys.

FIELD, ALEX. *Novelty Dances for Any Operetta*. New York: Music Publishers Holding Co., 1954.

GRAY, VERA, and PERCIVAL, RACHEL. *Music, Movement, and Mime*. New York: Oxford Pub., Co., 1965.

Excellent.

Handy Book of Folk Dances. Delaware, Ohio: Cooperative Recreation Service.

Excellent and inexpensive source for folk dancing.

HAYES, ELIZABETH R. *Introduction to the Teaching of Dance*. New York: The Ronald Press Co., 1964.

Excellent book in the creative teaching of fundamental movement, modern, folk, and ballroom dancing.

HOOD, MARGUERITE V. *Teaching Rhythm and Using Classroom Instruments*. Englewood Cliffs, N. J.: Prentice-Hall, Inc., 1970.

HUMPHREYS, LOUISE, and ROSS, JERROLD. *Interpreting Music Through Movement*. Englewood Cliffs, N. J.: Prentice-Hall, Inc., 1964.

Analysis of several works by well-known composers. Teaching suggestions included.

KULBITSKY, OLGA, and KALTMAN, FRANK L. *Teachers' Dance Handbook*. New York: Bluebird Pub. Co., 1959.

LaSalle, Dorothy. *Rhythms and Dances for Elementary Schools.* Rev. ed. New York: A. S. Barnes & Co., 1951.

Musical accompaniments and teaching suggestions for fundamental movement, dramatization, singing games, and dances. A standard reference for elementary teachers.

Latchaw, Marjorie, and Pyatt, Jean. *A Pocket Guide of Dance Activities.* Englewood Cliffs, New Jersey: Prentice-Hall Inc., 1958.

Small, practical, spiral-bound book of lesson suggestions using the experiences of children as sources for movement.

Materials for Teaching Dance. 3 vols. Prepared by the National Section on Dance, American Association for Health, Physical Education, and Recreation. Washington, D. C.: National Education Association, 1953-55.

Series of three booklets containing lists of recordings, piano music, and books: 1. "Modern Dance and Children's Dance"; 2. "Folk, Square, and Social Dance"; 3. "Selected Visual Aids for Dance."

Murray, Ruth Lovell. *Dance in Elementary Education.* 2nd ed. New York: Harper & Row, Pub., 1963.

Practical text and excellent source for all phases of dance activity for young children.

Saffran, Rosanna B. *First Book of Creative Rhythms.* New York: Holt, Rinehart & Winston, Inc., 1963.

Book on early rhythmic activities with particular emphasis on fundamental movement. Good source for classroom teachers in the lower grades.

Sehon, Elizabeth, and O'Brien, Emma Lou. *Rhythms in Elementary Education.* New York: A. S. Barnes & Co., 1951.

Text for teacher reference on techniques and materials.

Sheehy, Emma Dickson. *Children Discover Music and Dance.* New York: Henry Holt and Company, Inc., 1959.

Square Dance. Delaware, Ohio: Cooperative Recreation Service.

Calls and figures from original American folk sources.

II. Recordings

American Game and Activity Songs. Pete Seeger, Folkways #7002, (LCR-62-1498).

Especially for very young children.

Canadian Folk Dances, selected and edited by Eileen Reid, Bowmar Educational Records.

Recordings of Canadian Dances; instructions included.

Dances of Hawaii, Bowmar Educational Records. Nine ancient and modern dances of the South Seas.

Directions and information in separate booklet.

Dubka, Rashid Records, 191 Atlantic Ave., Brooklyn N.Y. 11201.

Music and dance directions for Middle-Eastern dancing.

Eight Swiss Dances, Paxton Records, PR 711 (Nos. 104), PR 712 (Nos. 5-8).

Instrumental ensemble performing the dances in the book by Desmond MacMahon. Dance instructions included.

Eighth 18th-Century Dances, Paxton Records PR 699 (Nos. 1-4), PR 700 (Nos. 5-88.

Recorded music and dance instructions for the dances in the book by Desmond MacMahon. Orchestration uses some instruments of the period, such as harpsichord and recorder.

Festival Folk Dances, RCA, (LPM-1621).

Includes the Highland fling, hornpipe, and ribbon dance. For older students.

First Folk Dances, RCA (LPM-1625).

Includes Polly Wolly Doodle, Kinderpolka, The Wheat, Dance of Greeting. For ages 5-8.

Folk Dances for All Ages, RCA (LPM-1622).

Grade 5 and up. Includes an excellent schottische and the "Norwegian Mountain March."

Folk Dances for Fun, RCA (LPM-1624), and *All-Purpose Folk Dances,* (LPM-1623).

Two companion albums to *First Folk Dances.* For grade 3 and up.

Folk Dance Records, Ruth Evans, Children's World, Inc., Box 433 Highland Station, Springfield, Mass. 01109.

Series of four albums with music and spoken directions for folk dances from many parts of America and western Europe.

Folkraft Records, 1159 Broad Street, Newark, New Jersey 07102.

Series of musical recordings suitable for folk dance accompaniment. International.

French Game Songs, Bowmar Educational Records, M-107.

One 12″ LP recording of the songs in the book by Ruth DeCesare (see under Music and Dance Collections).

Happy Folk Dances, RCA (LPM-1620). Folk dances for children of junior high school age.

Latin-American Game Songs, Bowmar Educational Records, M-104.

One 12″ LP recording of songs in the book by Ruth DeCesare (see under Music and Dance Collection).

Let's Square Dance, Richard Kraus, RCA Series 3000-3004.

Five albums beginning with fundamental steps (8-10 years) and increasing in difficulty. Fully illustrated instructions with each album. A "how-to-do-it" series.

Listen, Move, and Dance, Vols. 1 and 2, Capital Records, H-21006 and H-21007.

Mexican Folk Dances, Bowmar Educational Records.

Six popular Mexican dances with printed instructions included.

Play Party Games, Decca Records, AL278.

Favorite and familiar singing games such as "Skip to my Lou."

Play Party Games, Bowmar Educational Records.

Two albums of three records each containing many traditional singing games. Written instructions included.

Ring Around the Rosy and Other Singing Games, Allegro Records, JR-3.

Traditional songs and games for preschool and kindergarten.

Rhythms for Children (Call and Response). Ella Jenkins, Folkways (FC7308).

Group singing and drum rhythms with a group of children. Rhythm chants included.

Singing Games and Folk Dances, Bowmar Educational Records.

A series of albums (revised ed.) for young people.
Singing Games, Albums 1 and 2.
Singing Games and Folk Dances, Album 3.
Folk Dances, (from around the world), Album 4.
Folk Dances, (American) Album 5.
Folk Dances, (Latin-American), Album 6.

Singing Square Dances, Bowmar Educational Records.

Three albums with verbal instructions before each dance and a "singing" caller with the music. For grades 4 through junior high.

Sometime-Anytime Songs, Washington Records, (WC-303).

Refreshing, imaginative songs and musical interludes for response by very young children. Excellent for dramatizations.

Songs and Rhythms from Near and Far, Folkways #7655 (LCR-64-343).

Original songs in English by Ella Jenkins introducing folk rhythms from Canada, Greece, Syria, etc.

Square Dancing Made Easy, Columbia LN 3607.

Fourteen dances with detailed directions and square dance terms printed on record jacket.

Square Dances, Folkways #2001 (LCR-58-728).

Calls and music to both Eastern and Western Dances.

The World of Folk Dances, Michael Herman, RCA.

A series of seven albums, each with music played by a dance orchestra, and a teacher's manual with excellent dance directions.

First Folk Dances, LPM-1625 (5-8 years).
Folk Dances for Fun, LPM-1625 (8 years and up).
All Purpose Folk Dances, LPM-1623 (8 years and up).
Folk Dances for All Ages, LPM-1622 (10 years and up).
Festival Folk Dances, LPM-1621 (10 years and up).
Happy Folk Dances, LPM-1620 (12 years and up).
Special Folk Dances, LPM-1619.

Classified Listing of Musical Resources

AUDIO-VISUAL AIDS EQUIPMENT

Audio House, 307 E. 9th St., Lawrence, Kan. 6604

Bowmar Records, Inc., 622 Rodier Drive, Glendale, Calif. 91201

Stanley Bowmar Co., Inc., 4 Broadway, Valhalla, N.Y. 10595

Century Records Mfg. Co.—Century Custom Recording Service, P.O. Box 308, Squgus, Calif. 91350

Chesterfield Music Shops, Inc., 12 Warren St., New York, N.Y. 10007

Children's Music Center, Inc., 5373 West Pico Blvd., Los Angeles, Calif. 90019

Crest Records, Inc., 220 Broadway, Huntington Station, N.Y. 11746

Custom Fidelity Record Co., 222 E. Glenarm St., Pasadena, Calif. 91101

Folkways Records, 701—7th Ave., New York, N.Y. 10036

Herco Products, Inc., 53 W. 23rd St., New York, N.Y. 10010

Ken-Del Productions, Inc., Custom Record Division, 111 Valley Road—Richardson Park, Wilmington, Del. 19804

RCA Records, 1133 Ave. of the Americas, New York, N.Y. 10036

Radio-Matic of America, Inc., 760 Ramsey Ave., Hillside, N. J. 07205

Society for Visual Education, Inc., 1345 Diversey Parkway, Chicago, Ill. 60614

Vogt Quality Recordings, P.O. Box 302, Needham, Mass. 02192

BAND & ORCHESTRA INSTRUMENT MANUFACTURERS

W. T. Armstrong Company, Inc., 200 E. Sycamore St., Elkhart, Ind. 46514

Artley, Inc., P.O. Box 2280, Nogales, Ariz. 85621

C. Bruno & Son, Inc., 55 Marcus Drive, Melville, N.Y. 11746
    3443 E. Commerce St., San Antonio, Texas 78206
    5720 Union Pacific Ave., Los Angeles, Calif. 90022

Conn Corporation, 1101 East Beordsley, Elkhart, Ind. 46514

Fender Musical Instruments, CBS Musical Instruments, 1300 East Valencia, Fullerton, Calif. 92631

Fox Products Corp., South Whitley, Ind. 46787

K. G. Gemeinhardt Co., Inc., P.O. Box 788, Rt. 19, South Elkhart, Ind. 46514

Getzen Company, Inc., 211 W. Centralia St., Elkhorn, Wis. 53121

Goya Music, Div. of Avnet, Inc., 53 W. 23rd St., New York, N.Y. 10010

Wm. R. Gratz, Co., Inc., 14 Bixley Heath, Lynbrook, N.Y. 11563

The Fred Gretsch Co., Inc., 60 Broadway, Brooklyn, N.Y. 11211

Hargail Music, Inc., 157 W. 57th St., New York, N.Y. 10019

G. C. Jenkins Co., P.O. Box 2221, Decatur, Ill. 62526

Kelischek Workshop for Historical Instruments, 386 Allendale Drive, S.E., Atlanta, Ga. 30317

King Musical Instruments, 33999 Curtis Blvd., Eastlake, Ohio 44094

G. LeBlanc Corporation, 7019 30th Ave., Kenosha, Wis. 53141

William Lewis & Sons, 7390 N. Lincoln Ave., Lincolnwood, Ill. 60646

The Linton Company Inc., 711 Middleton Run Road, Elkhart, Ind. 46514

Ludwig Industries, 1728 N. Damen Ave., Chicago, Ill. 60647

Martin Band Instruments, DeKalb, Ill. 60115

Meinl-Weston Musical Instrument Company, 35 N. Ayer St., Harvard, Ill. 60033

C. Meisel Music Co., Subsidiary of Avnet, Inc., 2332 Morris Ave., Union, N. J. 07083

Mirafone Corporation, 1239 S. Olive, Los Angeles, Calif. 90015

Musser-Kitching—Div. Ludwig Industries, 505 Shawest, La Grange, Ill. 60525

F. E. Olds & Son, Inc., 350 S. Raymond Ave., Fullerton, Calif. 92631

Polisi Bassoon Corp., 244 W. 49th Street, New York, N.Y. 10019

G. Pruefer Mfg. Co., Inc., 185 Union Avenue, Providence, R. I. 02909

F. A. Reynolds Co., 5520 N. First Street, Abilene, Texas 79603

Rogers Drums, CBS Musical Instruments, 1300 East Valencia, Fullerton, California 92631

Walter E. Sear, 118 West 57th Street, New York, N.Y. 10019

Selmer—Division of Magnovox, Box 310, Elkhart, Indiana 46514

Scherl & Roth Incorporated, 1729 Superior Avenue, Cleveland, Ohio 44114

Schilke Music Products, Inc., 529 S. Wabash Avenue, Chicago, Illinois 60605

Slingerland Drum Co., 6633 N. Milwaukee Avenue, Niles, Illinois 60648

Vincent Bach Corp., 1119 N. Main, Box 377, Elkhart, Indiana 46514

Avedis Zildjian Company, 39 Fayette St., North Quincy, Mass. 02171

BAND UNIFORM AND CHOIR GOWN MANUFACTURERS

Bandribbons, Monmouth, Oregon 97361

Collegiate Cap and Gown Company, 1000 No. Market Street, Champaign, Ill. 61820

DeMoulin Bros. & Co., 1083 S. Fourth, Greenville, Illinois 62246

The Fechheimer Bros. Co., 4545 Malsbary Road, Cincinnati, Ohio 45242

Sol Frank Uniforms, Inc., 702 South Santa Rosa St., San Antonio, Texas 78207

Fruhauf Southwest Uniform Company, 312 East English Street, Wichita, Kansas 67202

Robert Rollins Blazers, Inc., 242 Park Avenue, South, New York, N.Y. 10003

"Uniforms By Ostwald," Inc., Ostwald Plaza, Box No. 70, Staten Island, New York 10314

The C. E. Ward Company, New London, Conn. 44851

MUSIC TEXTBOOK PUBLISHERS

Allyn and Bacon, Inc., 470 Atlantic Avenue, Boston Mass. 02210

American Book Company, 430 West 33rd Street, New York, N.Y. 10001

Appleton-Century-Crofts, Educational Division of Meredith Corp., 440 Park Avenue, South, New York, N.Y. 10016

William C. Brown Company Publishers, 135 S. Locust Street, Dubuque, Iowa 52001

Follett Educational Corporation, 1010 W. Washington Blvd., Chicago, Illinois 60607

Ginn and Company, Statler Building, Boston, Mass. 02117

Holt, Rinehart and Winston, Inc., 383 Madison Avenue, New York, New York 10017

Prentice-Hall, Inc., Englewood Cliffs, N. J. 07632

Silver-Burdett Co., Morristown, New Jersey 07960

Wadsworth Publishing Company, Inc., 10 Davis Drive, Belmont, California 94002

MUSICAL EQUIPMENT MANUFACTURERS

Bela Seating Company, Inc., 9505 South Prairie Avenue, Chicago, Illinois 60628

Clarin Corporation, 4640 West Harrison Street, Chicago, Illinois 60644

The Empire Music Company, Ltd., 934—12th Street, New Westminster, B. C., Canada

Krauth and Benninghofen, Inc., 3001 Symmes Road, Hamilton, Ohio 45012

Magnamusic-Baton, Inc., 6390 Delmar Blvd., St. Louis, Mo. 63130

Manhassett Specialty Co., P.O. Box 2518, Yakima, Washington 98902
Melody Cradle Company, 1502 South Twelfth Street, Goshen, Indiana 46526
Mitchell Manufacturing Co., 2740 South 34th Street, Milwaukee, Wisconsin 53246
Pacific Music Papers, 1309 No. Highland Avenue, Hollywood, California 90028
Pacific Music Supply Co., 1143 Santee Street, Los Angeles, Calif. 90015
Peripole Products, Inc., 51-17 Rockaway Beach Blvd., Rockaway, L. I., N.Y. 11691
B. Portnoy Clarinet Accessories, 1715 Circle Drive, Bloomington, Indiana 47401
Rabco "ReeDuAl," Inc., P.O. Box 782, North Miami, Fla. 33161
Remo, Inc., 12804 Raymer Street, North Hollywood, Calif. 91605
Rhythm Band, Incorporated, P.O. Box 126, Forth Worth, Texas 76101
Rico Corporation, P.O. Box 5028, Bendix Station, N. Hollywood, Calif. 91605
Oscar Schmidt-International, Inc., Garden State Road, Union, N. J. 07083
School Specialties, 48 W. Northfield Rd., Livingston, N. J. 07039
Schulmerich Carillons, Inc., Carillon Hill, Sellersville, Pa. 18960
Trophy Music Company, Div. of Grossman Music Corp., 1278 West 9th Street, Cleveland, Ohio 44113
Wenger Corporation, 90 Park Drive, Owatonna, Minn. 55060

PIANO AND ORGAN MANUFACTURERS

Baldwin Piano & Organ Company, 1801 Gilbert Avenue, Cincinnati, Ohio 45202
Conn Organ Corp., 1101 East Beardsley, Elkhart, Ind. 46514
    Deerfield, Mass. 01373
Hammond Organ Company, 4200 West Diversey Avenue, Chicago, Illinois 60639
M. Hohner, Inc., Andrews Road, Hicksville, L. I., N.Y. 11802
Lowrey Organ & Piano Company, 7373 N. Cicero Avenue, Lincolnwood, Illinois 60646
Steinway & Sons, Steinway Place, Long Island City, N.Y. 11105
Story & Clark Piano Co., 7373 N. Cicero Avenue, Lincolnwood, Ill. 60646
The Wurlitzer Company, DeKalb, Illinois 60115

Musical Activities Related to the Treatment of Mobility, Endurance, and Coordination Problems

JOINT AND RELATED MUSCLE GROUPS	SPECIFIC MUSIC THERAPY ACTIVITY
1. NECK	
Flexors (move head forward)	Piano and other Keyboard Instruments (high seating arrangement)
	Mallett Instruments
	Marimba (high seating arrangement)
	Vibraharp (high seating arrangement)
Extensors (move head back)	Singing
	Woodwind Instruments
	Brass Instruments
Lateral Flexors (move head to side)	String Instruments
	Violin
	Viola
2. TRUNK	
Flexor	String Instruments
	Cello
	Bass Viol
	Percussion Instruments
	Tympani
	Bass Drum
3. HIP	
Flexors (move thigh up)	Keyboard and Harp Instruments
	Piano—pedalling (high seating arrangement at first; gradually lower)
	Organ—pedalling (high seating arrangement at first; gradually lower)
	Harp—pedalling (high seating arrangement at first; gradually lower)
Extensors (move thigh down)	Keyboard Instruments
	Piano—pedalling, tight-action pedal as resistance against gravity (low seating arrangement at first; gradually higher)
	Organ—pedalling (low seating arrangement at first; gradually higher)

This muscle chart is based on the "Muscle Examination Chart" of the National Foundation for Infantile Paralysis. The basis for the listing on dental formations is from the work of Dr. Howard E. Kessler, "Dental Changes produced by the Playing of Musical Wind Instruments," *Dental Survey*, Jan., 1956. Many of the musical activities in this may be adapted for use in increasing endurance and strength of muscle groups. For example, certain instruments (or parts of instruments) may be redesigned in heavier materials so that greater activity becomes a strongly resistive one.

4. KNEE

Flexors (inner and outer ham-string muscles)

Keyboard Instruments
    Piano—pedalling (best when hip is well flexed; high seating arrangement at first; gradually lower)

Extensors

Keyboard Instruments
    Piano—pedalling; tight-action pedal as resistance against gravity (low seating arrangement at first; gradually higher)

5. ANKLE

Plantar-flexors (Gastroc and Soeleus—Ball of foot down when knee is extended)

Keyboard Instruments
    Piano—pedalling (best when knee is held in extension in moderately high seating position)
    Organ—swell pedal
    Player Piano—treadling

Percussion Instruments
    Bass Drum—pedal mechanism (also available are foot volume and tone controls)
    Maracas—pedal operated

6. FOOT

Invertors (Anterior and Posterior Tilvialis)

Keyboard and Harp Instruments
    Piano—pedalling (foot inverted)
    Harp—pedalling (foot inverted)

Evertors (Peroneus Brevis and Longus)

Keyboard and Harp Instruments
    Piano—pedalling (foot inverted)
    Harp—pedalling (foot inverted)

Percussion Instruments
    Bass Drum (foot volumne and tone controls)
    Maracas—pedal operated (foot everted)

7. SCAPULA (shoulder blade)

Abductor (Serratus Anterior)

Keyboard and Harp Instruments
    Piano (cross-hand passage work)
    Harp
    Accordion
    Concertina

String Instruments
    Cello
    Bass Viol

Mallet Played Instruments
    Marimba (cross-hand passage work or the equivalent)

Adductors (Middle Trapezius and Rhomboids—move shoulder blades toward each other)

Keyboard and Harp Instruments
    Piano (move four middle register to extreme registers of keyboard bilaterally)
    Harp
    Accordion
    Concertina

String Instruments
    Cello
    Bass Viol

Woodwind Instruments
    Saxophone
    Bassoon

Elevators

Keyboard Instruments
   Accordion
   Concertina
String Instruments
   Violin
   Viol
Woodwind Instruments
   Bassoon
Brass Instruments
   Trombone

Stabilizing Function

Any instrument which can be placed up high in order to bring the scapular muscles into a position of strongest stabilization.

8. SHOULDER

Flexors (arm forward at shoulder joint)

Mallet Played Instruments
   Marimba
   Vibraharp
Percussion Instruments
   Drums (use heavy drumsticks to counteract pull of gravity)
Baton—conducting

Abductors (arm up and out to side)

Keyboard Instruments
   Accordion
Mallet Played Instruments
   Vertical Chimes (place patient so he stands with affected side toward chimes)

Horizontal Abductor

Keyboard Instruments
   Accordion
   Piano (use music containing scale and/or arpeggio passage work, or chords which move from middle register to extreme registers of keyboard)
String Instruments
   Violin
   Viola
   Cello
Percussion Instruments
   Cymbals

Horizontal Adductor

Keyboard Instruments
   Piano (use music containing scale and/or arpeggio passage work, or chords which move from extreme registers of keyboard to middle register)
   Accordion
   Concertina
String Instruments
   Violin
   Viola
   Cello
Mallett Played Instruments
Vibraharp
Baton—conducting

External Rotators

Toy Instruments
Percussion Instruments
   Melody Bells
Keyboard Instruments
   Piano—glissando passages with thumb

Internal Rotators

Toy Instruments
Percussion Instruments
Keyboard Instruments

9. ELBOW

Flexors

Plectrum Instruments
    Autoharp
    Guitar
    Banjo
    Mandolin
String Instruments
    Violin
    Viola
    Cello
Woodwind Instruments
    Clarinet
    Oboe
    English Horn
Keyboard and Harp Instruments
    Piano (slow playing, with emphasis on contraction and immediate relaxation of the Biceps with some shoulder depression by Triceps. Good for muscle strengthening at that joint—not for range of motion. Grade by means of gradually increasing volume of tone patient produces)
    Accordion
    Concertina
    Harp
Brass Instruments
    Trombone
Percussion Instruments
    Cymbals
    Sand Blocks
    Rhythm Sticks

Extensors

    Autoharp
    Guitar
    Ukulele
    Banjo
String Instruments
    Violin
    Viola
    Cello
    Bass Viol
Woodwind Instruments
    Clarinets
    Oboe
    English Horn
Keyboard and Harp Instruments
    Accordion
    Concertina
Brass Instruments
    Trombone
Percussion Instruments
    Rhythm Sticks
    Tambourine

10. FOREARM

Supinators (rotate forearm to turn palm up)

Keyboard Instruments
Piano (use music containing arpeggios in contrary motion, broken in each hand from the thumb toward the fifth finger)
Organ (dials)
Accordion (buttons and bellows)

Percussion Instruments
Tambourine
Dumbbell Maracas

Plectrum Instruments
Autoharp
Guitar
Banjo
Mandolin

Pronators (rotate forearm to turn palm down)

Keyboard Instruments
Piano (use music containing arpeggios in contrary motion)
Organ (dials)
Accordion (bellows)

Percussion Instruments

Plectrum Instruments

11. WRIST

Flexor (with radial deviation toward thumb of hand or with ulnar deviation toward 5th finger side of hand)

Plectrum Instruments
Keyboard Instruments
Brass Instruments
Trumpet (manipulating a mute device)
Percussion Instruments

Extensors (with radial deviation toward thumb side of hand or with ulnar deviation toward 5th finger of hand)

Plectrum Instruments
Brass Instruments
Trumpet (valves)
Woodwind Instruments
Percussion Instruments
Triangle
Bongo Drums (no sticks)
Keyboard Instruments

12. FINGERS

Flexors (metacarpophalangeal—bend at joint nearest wrist; known as MP joints)

Keyboard Instruments
Piano (legato passage work)
Brass Instruments
Plectrum Instruments
Percussion Instruments
Woodwind Instruments

Extensors (metacarpophalangeal; MP joints)

Plectrum Instruments
Autoharp (pressing bars)
Guitar
Banjo

Keyboard and Harp Instruments
Piano (octave and large cord work)
Chord Organ (pressing buttons wtih left hand; keys on manual with right hand)
Harp

Woodwind Instruments
Clarinet
Oboe
Saxophone

Percussion Instruments

Flexors (proximal interphalangeal—bend at joint second from wrist; known as IP joints)

Plectrum Instruments
Woodwind Instruments
    Recorder (stabilize MP joints)
Brass Instruments
    Clarinet (stabilize MP joints)
Keyboard and Harp Instruments
    Piano (sliding grace-note game or piece in which each finger slides from black key to adjacent white key. May stabilize MP joint by having palm of hand rest on wood rim under keyboard.)
    Organ
    Harp

Flexors (distal interphalangeal—bend at joint third from wrist; IP joints)

Plectrum Instruments
Woodwind Instruments
Brass Instruments
Keyboard and Harp Instruments
    Piano (see exercise above)

Abductors (spread fingers apart)

Keyboard and Harp Instruments
    Piano (wide chord work; or legato passages involving large stretches between fingers)
    Accordion
    Harp
    Organ
Woodwind Instruments
    Recorder (vertical flute)
    Clarinet
    Oboe
Percussion Instruments
    Castanets
    Finger Cymbals
Plectrum Instruments
    Guitar
    Ukulele
    Banjo

Adductors

Keyboard and Harp Instruments
    Piano (passages in which thumb holds note, and other fingers move in toward it note-by-note)
    Organ
    Harp
Percussion Instruments
Plectrum Instruments

Opponens (5th finger rotates inward to touch thumb)

Keyboard Instruments
    Piano (passage work in which thumb holds note and 5th finger moves in to play adjacent notes)
Percussion Instruments
    Finger Cymbals (attached to thumb and to 5th finger; keep thumb stationary)

13. GROSS GRASP WITH FINGERS AND THUMB

Toy Instruments (Miniature animals which are activated to play the instruments they hold by means of a squeeze bulb attached to a rubber tube fastened to the animal, e.g., a monkey with cymbals, monkey with a drum, elephant with drum and cymbals.

14. THUMB

Opponens (thumb moves to touch any of the other fingers with an upwardly rotating motion)

Keyboard Instruments
  Piano (passage work in which 5th finger holds note and thumb moves in to play adjacent of melody)
  Organ
Percussion Instruments

Flexor (metacarpophalangeal—bend at joint nearest wrist)

Keyboard Instruments
  Piano

15. FACIAL MUSCLES

Singing (relaxed "ah" vocalizing with lullaby or similarly soothing music)
Wind Instruments

16. PALATAL MUSCLES

Singing (relaxed "ah" vocalizing with lullaby or similarly soothing music)

17. LARYNGEAL MUSCLES

Singing (Vocalized sighs resulting in an "a" hum; humming to soothing appealing music)
Wind Instruments

18. RESPIRATORY MUSCLES AND LUNGS

Diaphragm (emphasis should be on maximum increase of diaphragmatic rather than intercostal breathing)

Wind Instruments
Rhythmic Breathing (to musical jingles, with music so adjusted that expiration phase is longer than inspiration phase. Upper portion of thorax should be kept as immobile as possible in order to increase "abdominal breathing")
Singing (diaphragmatic action)

19. MOUTH AND DENTAL FORMATIONS

Class II Type of Malocclusion

Brass Instruments
  Trumpets
  Cornet
  Bugle
  Tuba
Woodwind Instruments
  Flute
  Piccolo
  Oboe
  Bassoon

Class III Type of Malocclusion

Woodwind Instruments
  Clarinet
  Saxophone
  Bassoon

Lists of Songs for Group Singing

BROTHERHOOD

Born Free
Dona Nobis Pacem
Faith of Our Fathers
God of Our Fathers
He's Got the Whole World In His Hands
It's a Small, Small World
Kum Ba Yah, My Lord

Let There Be Peace on Earth
Michael Row Your Boat
This Land Is Your Land
Vive L'Amour
What the World Needs Now
Let Us Break Bread Together

CAMPFIRE

Abide With Me
All Night All Day
All Through the Night
Aura Lee
Billy Boy
Deep River
Down in the Valley
Goodbye Old Paint
Good Night Ladies
Hey Ho Nobody
Home on the Range
In the Evening by the Moonlight
Jacob's Ladder
Kum Ba Yah, My Lord

Lone Prairie
My Bonnie Lies Over the Ocean
Now the Day Is Over
Oh Dear, What Can the Matter Be?
Old Texas
On Top of Old Smoky
Red River Valley
She'll Be Comin' Round the Mountain
So Long
Streets of Laredo
Sweet and Low
Taps (Day Is Done)
Tell Me Why
There's a Long, Long Trail

COMBINED SONGS

(These songs, when sung simultaneously, can provide
  a satisfying experience with harmony)
Are You Sleeping—Farmer in the Dell
A Spanish Cavalier—Solomon Levi
Keep the Home Fires Burning—Long, Long Trail
Lazy Mary Will You Get Up—London Bridge
Lone Star Trail—Old Texas
Mary Had a Little Lamb—Oh, Dear, What Can the
  Matter Be?

My Home's in Montana—Home on the Range
Ring, Ring the Banjo—The Girl I Left Behind Me
Rock-a-My Soul—Ten Little Indians
Row Row Row Your Boat—Three Blind Mice
Sweetly Sings the Donkey—Where Is John?
Swing Low—All Through the Night

FUN AND NONSENSE

Bicycle Built for Two
Bingo
Blue Tail Fly
Boola-Boola
Camptown Races
Chumbara
Clementine
Deep in the Heart of Texas
Did You Ever See a Lassie?
Dinah
Do-Re-Mi
Down by the Station
Five Foot Two
For He's a Jolly Good Fellow
Hole in the Bucket
How Do You "Mr. ...."
If You're Happy and You Know It
I'm a Yankee Doodle Dandy
It Ain't Gonna Rain No More
John Jacob Jinkle Heimer Schmidt
La Cucuracha
Lazy Mary Will You Get Up

Li'l Liza Jane
By Bonnie Lies Over the Ocean
Oh Susannah
Oh Where, Oh Where Has My Little Dog Gone?
Old King Cole
Old MacDonald Had a Farm
Paper of Pins
Raindrops Keep Falling on My Head
Reuben & Rachel
Sarasponda
Shoo Fly
Skip to My Lou
Ta-Ra-Ra-Boom-de-ay
Ten Little Indians
The Keeper
The More We Get Together
There's a Tavern in the Town
This Old Man
While Strolling Through the Park One Day
Whistle a Happy Tune
Zulu Warrior

HERITAGE SONGS

Blow the Man Down
Carry Me Back to Old Virginny
Casey Jones
Clementine
Dixie
East Side, West Side
Erie Canal
God Bless America
God of Our Fathers
I've Been Workin' on the Railroad

Oh Susannah
Old Folks at Home
Red River Valley
Shenandoah
Streets of Laredo
Sweet Betsy from Pike
Swing Low, Sweet Chariot
This Is My Country
Yankee Doodle

HIKING

Across the Plain
A-Hunting We Will Go
Air Force Song
Anchors Aweigh
Battle Hymn of the Republic
Deep in the Heart of Texas
Don't Fence Me In
I've Been Working on the Railroad
I've Got Sixpence
Loch Lomond
Marching Along Together
Marching to Pretoria
Marines' Hymn
Oh Susannah
Onward Christian Soldiers

Sailing, Sailing
Stout Hearted Men
The Army Goes Rolling Along
The Campbells Are Coming
The Happy Wanderer
The Upward Trail
Vive L'Amour
Walking at Night
Waltzing Matilda
When Johnny Comes Marching Home Again
When the Saints Go Marching In
Yankee Doodle
You're a Grand Old Flag
Zum Gali Gali

HOLIDAY SONGS

Angels We Have Heard on High
Away in a Manger

O Come All Ye Faithful
O Little Town of Bethlehem

Bring a Torch Jeanette Isabella
Come Ye Thankful People Come
Easter Parade
Greensleeves
Happy Birthday to You
I'm Dreaming of a White Christmas
Jingle Bells
Joy to the World

Over the River and Through the Woods
Prayer of Thanksgiving
Silent Night
The First Noel
Up on the Housetop
We Three Kings
We Wish You a Merry Christmas

RELIGIOUS

All Night All Day
Deep River
Do Lord
Dona Nobis Pacem
Doxology
Everytime I Feel the Spirit
Fairest Lord Jesus
For the Beauty of the Earth
Go Down Moses
Golden Slippers
He's Got the Whole World in His Hands
I'm Goin' to Sing When the Spirit Says Sing

Jacob's Ladder
Joshua Fought the Battle of Jericho
Kum Ba Yah, My Lord
Michael Row Your Boat
Nobody Knows the Trouble I've Seen
Old Hundred
Prayer of Thanksgiving
Rock of Ages
Steal Away
Swing Low Sweet Chariot
Were You There?
When Jesus Wept

ROUNDS

Alouette
Dona Nobis Pacem
For Health and Strength
French Cathedral Bell Round
Hey Ho Nobody Home
Kookaburra
Little Tom Tinker
Make New Friends

Music Alone Shall Live
Oh How Lovely Is the Evening
Scotland's Burning
Shalom Chaverim
Streets of Laredo
Sweetly Sings the Donkey
White Coral Bells

SENTIMENTAL

After the Ball Is Over
All Through the Night
Aloha Oe
Ashgrove
Auld Lang Syne
Believe Me If All Those Endearing Young Charms
Bells of St. Mary
Carry Me Back to Old Virginny
Cielito Lindo
Dear Hearts and Gentle People
Down by the Old Mill Stream
Down in the Valley
Drink to Me Only with Thine Eyes
Five Hundred Miles
Flow Gently Sweet Afton
Goodbye Old Paint

Keep the Home Fires Burning
Let Me Call You Sweetheart
Little Mohee
Long, Long Ago
Oh What a Beautiful Morning
Old Folks at Home
Red River Valley
Santa Lucia
Shenandoah
Sing Your Way Home
So Long
Sweet and Low
Tell Me Why
There's a Long, Long Trail
Wait Till the Sun Shines Nellie
Where Have All the Flowers Gone

MT87 .B4
Batcheller, John
Music in recreation and leisur
c.1
100106 000

3 9310 00063338 6
GOSHEN COLLEGE-GOOD LIBRARY